HOMEMADE DOG FOOD RECIPE BOOK

QUANTITIES FOR:
PUPPIES
ADULTS
SENIORS

Welcome to the "Homemade Dog Food Recipe Book", an essential guide for every dog lover who wishes to provide their furry friends with nutritious and delicious homemade meals. This comprehensive book is a treasure trove of culinary delights specifically tailored for dogs, featuring a diverse range of 75 recipes. Inside, you'll discover 25 recipes for wholesome dog meals, carefully crafted to ensure a balanced and healthy diet for your canine companion. Additionally, we have included 25 recipes for dog treats, perfect for training or simply spoiling your pup with some extra love. And for those special occasions, explore our 25 delectable dog cake recipes, guaranteed to make any tail wag with joy. Each recipe is easy to follow, uses readily available ingredients, and has been vet-approved to ensure they are safe and beneficial for your dog. Whether you're a seasoned dog owner or new to the world of homemade dog cuisine, this book is your go-to resource for feeding your dog with the best nature has to offer.

Consult your veterinarian or pet nutritionist to ensure these recipes are suitable for your dog's specific dietary needs.

He recommends that you change your dog's food gradually by replacing it with the current food, starting with 1/4 of the new food and 3/4 of the current one to begin with.
Then, little by little, increase the proportion until you replace the commercial food with the nutritious food.

DOG MEALS

DOG BISCUITS

DOG CAKES

HARMFUL AND TOXIC INGREDIENTS FOR DOGS

DOG MEALS

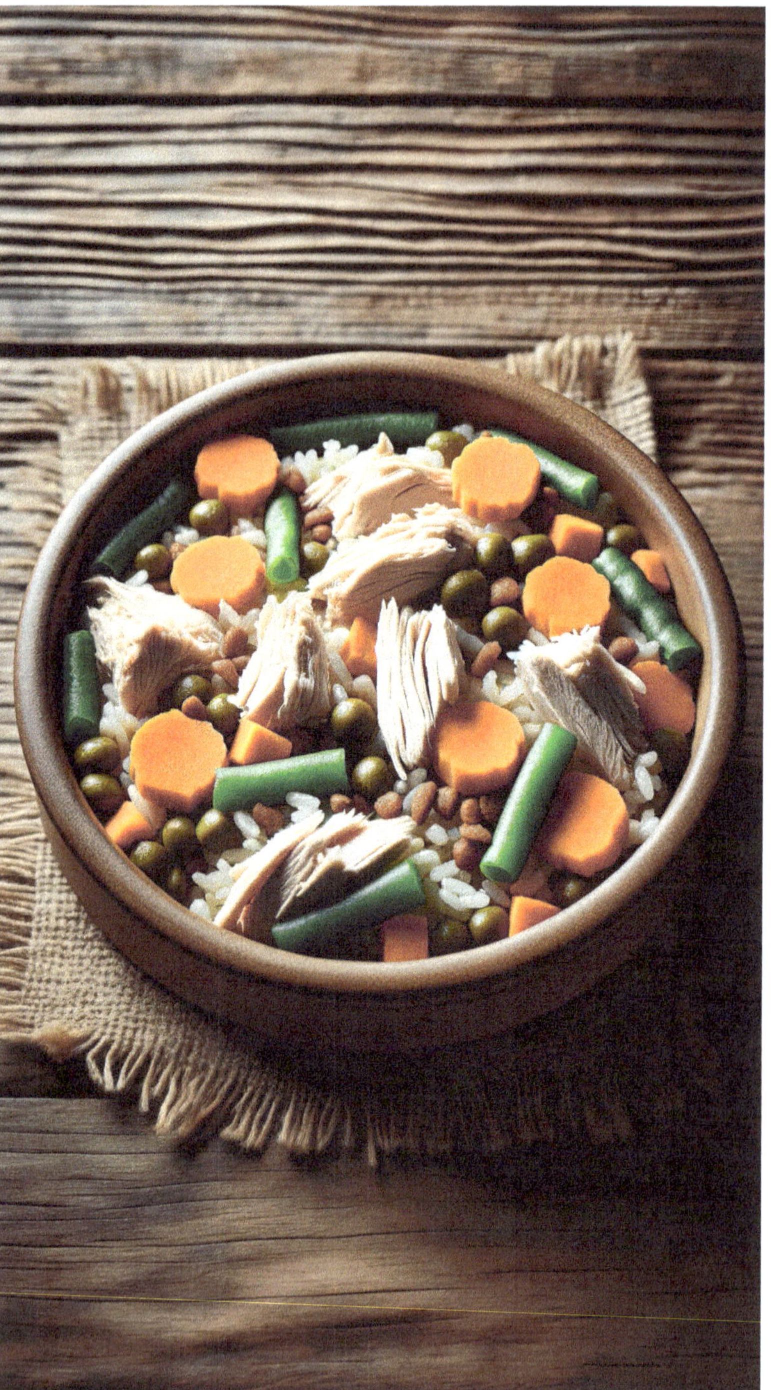

CHICKEN & VEGGIE DELIGHT

PREP
15 MIN

COOK
30 MIN

DIFFICULTY
EASY

INGREDIENTS AND QUANTITIES

Ingredients	Puppy (<6 months)	Adult (>6 months-7 years)	Senior (7+ years)
Boiled Chicken	50g - 1.76 oz	100g - 3.5 oz	80g - 2.8 oz
Brown Rice	50g - 1/4 cup	100g- 1/2 cup	75g - 1/3 cup
Carrots	1 small	2 small	1 medium
Green Beans	3-4 beans	5-7 beans	4-5 beans

METHOD

Cook the Chicken: Start by cooking the chicken breast thoroughly until no pink remains. Once cooked, dice it into small, bite-sized pieces suitable for your dog's size.

Prepare the Rice: Cook the brown rice as per the package instructions. Ensure it's fully cooked and soft.

Steam the Carrots: Cut carrots into small pieces and steam them until they are soft but not mushy.

Prepare the Spinach: Finely chop the spinach. You can steam it lightly if your dog prefers softer greens.

Combine and Serve: In your dog's bowl, arrange the chicken, rice, carrots, and spinach in separate sections for a visually appealing meal.

ADVICE

- Always ensure that the chicken is thoroughly cooked to eliminate harmful bacteria.
- Adjust portion sizes according to your dog's size and dietary needs.
- This meal provides a good balance of protein, carbohydrates, and essential nutrients.

SALMON AND RICE FEAST

PREP
20 MIN

COOK
30 MIN

DIFFICULTY
EASY

INGREDIENTS AND QUANTITIES

Ingredients	Puppy (<6 months)	Adult (>6 months-7 years)	Senior (7+ years)
Cooked salmon (boneless)	80g / 2.8oz	120g / 4.2oz	100g / 3.5oz
Brown rice	40g / 1.4oz	80g / 2.8oz	60g / 2.1oz
Broccoli	20g / 0.7oz	40g / 1.4oz	30g / 1oz
Peas	20g / 0.7oz	40g / 1.4oz	30g / 1oz

METHOD

Cook Salmon: Gently cook the salmon until it flakes easily. Be sure to remove all bones.

Cook Rice: Cook brown rice as per package instructions until it's soft.

Steam Vegetables: Steam broccoli and peas until they are tender.

Mix Together: Flake the salmon and mix it with the cooked rice, broccoli, and peas.

Cool Down: Let the mixture cool to room temperature before serving.

ADVICE

- Ensure that the salmon is fully cooked and boneless to prevent any choking hazards.

- Chop the broccoli and peas into small pieces to make them easier for your dog to eat and digest.

- Adjust portion sizes based on your dog's age, size, and activity level.

TURKEY PUMPKIN MEDLEY

PREP
15 MIN

COOK
25 MIN

DIFFICULTY
EASY

INGREDIENTS AND QUANTITIES

Ingredients	Puppy (<6 months)	Adult (>6 months-7 years)	Senior (7+ years)
Ground turkey (lean)	100g / 3.5oz	150g / 5.3oz	120g / 4.2oz
Pumpkin (mashed)	50g / 1.8oz	100g / 3.5oz	80g / 2.8oz
Zucchini	30g / 1oz	60g / 2.1oz	50g / 1.8oz
Quinoa (cooked)	40g / 1.4oz	80g / 2.8oz	60g / 2.1oz

METHOD

Cook Turkey: Brown the ground turkey in a pan until it's fully cooked.

Prepare Pumpkin: Mash cooked or canned pumpkin (ensure it's plain, without additives).

Chop Zucchini: Finely chop the zucchini.

Cook Quinoa: Cook quinoa according to package instructions.

Mix All Ingredients: Combine the turkey, pumpkin, zucchini, and quinoa in a bowl.

Serve: Cool the mixture to room temperature before serving.

ADVICE

- Always ensure that the chicken is thoroughly cooked to eliminate harmful bacteria.
- Adjust portion sizes according to your dog's size and dietary needs.
- This meal provides a good balance of protein, carbohydrates, and essential nutrients.

BEEF LIVER AND VEGGIE MIX

PREP
20 MIN

COOK
30 MIN

DIFFICULTY
EASY

INGREDIENTS AND QUANTITIES

Ingredients	Puppy (<6 months)	Adult (>6 months-7 years)	Senior (7+ years)
Beef liver	80g / 2.8oz	120g / 4.2oz	100g / 3.5oz
Brown rice	50g / 1.8oz	100g / 3.5oz	80g / 2.8oz
Kale	25g / 0.9oz	50g / 1.8oz	40g / 1.4oz
Carrots	25g / 0.9oz	50g / 1.8oz	40g / 1.4oz

METHOD

Cook Beef Liver: Cook the beef liver in a pan until it's fully cooked, then chop it into small pieces.

Cook Rice: Prepare brown rice according to package instructions.

Steam Vegetables: Steam kale and carrots until they are soft, then chop them finely.

Combine Ingredients: Mix the beef liver, brown rice, kale, and carrots together in a bowl.

Cool and Serve: Allow the food to cool to room temperature before serving to your dog.

ADVICE

- Make sure the beef liver is thoroughly cooked to eliminate any harmful bacteria.

- Finely chop the kale and carrots to aid in digestion and prevent choking.

- Adjust portion sizes to suit your dog's size and dietary needs.

CHICKEN OATS AND GREENS

PREP
20 MIN

COOK
30 MIN

DIFFICULTY
EASY

INGREDIENTS AND QUANTITIES

Ingredients	Puppy (<6 months)	Adult (>6 months-7 years)	Senior (7+ years)
Grilled chicken	100g / 3.5oz	150g / 5.3oz	120g / 4.2oz
Oats	30g / 1oz	60g / 2.1oz	50g / 1.8oz
Spinach	20g / 0.7oz	40g / 1.4oz	30g / 1oz
Blueberries	10g / 0.35oz	20g / 0.7oz	15g / 0.5oz

METHOD

Grill Chicken: Grill the chicken until fully cooked, then let it cool and chop into small pieces.

Cook Oats: Prepare oats as per package instructions.

Prepare Spinach and Blueberries: Lightly steam the spinach and rinse the blueberries.

Combine Ingredients: In a bowl, mix the grilled chicken, oats, spinach, and blueberries.

Serve: Ensure the meal is at room temperature before serving to your dog.

ADVICE

- Always make sure the chicken is thoroughly cooked to prevent any risk of bacterial infections.

- Chop spinach into small pieces to aid in digestion.

- Blueberries should be given in moderation due to their sugar content.

TURKEY AND BARLEY VEGGIE

PREP
20 MIN

COOK
40 MIN

DIFFICULTY
EASY

INGREDIENTS AND QUANTITIES

Ingredients	Puppy (<6 months)	Adult (>6 months-7 years)	Senior (7+ years)
Roasted turkey	100g / 3.5oz	150g / 5.3oz	120g / 4.2oz
Barley	50g / 1.8oz	100g / 3.5oz	80g / 2.8oz
Carrots	25g / 0.9oz	50g / 1.8oz	40g / 1.4oz
Peas	25g / 0.9oz	50g / 1.8oz	40g / 1.4oz
Green beans	25g / 0.9oz	50g / 1.8oz	40g / 1.4oz

METHOD

Roast Turkey: Roast the turkey until fully cooked, then shred it into small pieces.

Cook Barley: Prepare barley as per package instructions until it's tender.

Steam Vegetables: Steam carrots, peas, and green beans until they are soft.

Combine Ingredients: In a bowl, mix the roasted turkey, cooked barley, and steamed vegetables.

Serve: Let the mixture cool to room temperature before serving it to your dog.

ADVICE

- Ensure the turkey is thoroughly cooked to eliminate the risk of bacterial contamination.

- Chop the vegetables into small, digestible pieces.

- Adjust the portion size according to your dog's size and nutritional needs.

COD AND COUSCOUS VEGETABLE

PREP
20 MIN

COOK
30 MIN

DIFFICULTY
EASY

INGREDIENTS AND QUANTITIES

Ingredients	Puppy (<6 months)	Adult (>6 months-7 years)	Senior (7+ years)
Baked cod	80g / 2.8oz	120g / 4.2oz	100g / 3.5oz
Couscous	40g / 1.4oz	80g / 2.8oz	60g / 2.1oz
Pumpkin	30g / 1oz	60g / 2.1oz	50g / 1.8oz
Zucchini	30g / 1oz	60g / 2.1oz	50g / 1.8oz
Blueberries	20g / 0.7oz	40g / 1.4oz	30g / 1oz

METHOD

Bake Cod: Bake the cod in the oven until it's flaky. Ensure all bones are removed.

Cook Couscous: Prepare couscous according to package instructions.

Steam Vegetables: Steam diced pumpkin, sliced zucchini, and chopped bell peppers until tender.

Combine Ingredients: Mix the baked cod, couscous, and steamed vegetables in a bowl.

Cool and Serve: Allow the meal to cool to room temperature before serving.

ADVICE

- Make sure to remove all bones from the cod to prevent choking hazards.

- Chop the vegetables into small pieces for easier digestion.

- Balance the portion size according to your dog's age, size, and activity level.

LAMB AND MILLET VEGETABLE MIX

PREP
25 MIN

COOK
35 MIN

DIFFICULTY
EASY

INGREDIENTS AND QUANTITIES

Ingredients	Puppy (<6 months)	Adult (>6 months-7 years)	Senior (7+ years)
Roasted lamb	100g / 3.5oz	150g / 5.3oz	120g / 4.2oz
Millet	50g / 1.8oz	100g / 3.5oz	80g / 2.8oz
Beets	30g / 1oz	60g / 2.1oz	50g / 1.8oz
Asparagus	30g / 1oz	60g / 2.1oz	50g / 1.8oz
Butternut squash	30g / 1oz	60g / 2.1oz	50g / 1.8oz

METHOD

Roast Lamb: Roast the lamb until fully cooked, then chop it into small, bite-sized pieces.

Cook Millet: Prepare millet according to package instructions.

Steam Vegetables: Steam diced beets, chopped asparagus, and cubed butternut squash until tender.

Combine Ingredients: Mix the roasted lamb, cooked millet, and steamed vegetables in a bowl.

Serve: Ensure the meal is cooled to room temperature before serving to your dog.

ADVICE

- Ensure the lamb is well-cooked to avoid the risk of bacterial infections.

- Chop vegetables into small, digestible sizes.

- Adjust the portion size according to your dog's size and nutritional needs.

FISH AND RICE VEGGIE

PREP
15 MIN

COOK
25 MIN

DIFFICULTY
EASY

INGREDIENTS AND QUANTITIES

Ingredients	Puppy (<6 months)	Adult (>6 months-7 years)	Senior (7+ years)
Poached fish	80g / 2.8oz	120g / 4.2oz	100g / 3.5oz
White rice	50g / 1.8oz	100g / 3.5oz	80g / 2.8oz
Broccoli	20g / 0.7oz	40g / 1.4oz	30g / 1oz
Carrots	20g / 0.7oz	40g / 1.4oz	30g / 1oz
Peas	20g / 0.7oz	40g / 1.4oz	30g / 1oz

METHOD

Poach Fish: Gently poach the fish in water until it's fully cooked, then flake it, ensuring no bones remain.

Cook Rice: Prepare white rice according to package instructions.

Steam Vegetables: Steam broccoli, carrots, and peas until they are soft.

Combine Ingredients: In a bowl, mix the poached fish, cooked rice, and steamed vegetables.

Serve: Allow the mixture to cool to room temperature before serving.

ADVICE

- Ensure all bones are removed from the fish to prevent choking hazards.

- Cut the vegetables into small pieces for easy digestion.

- Balance the portion size based on your dog's size, age, and activity level.

GRILLED TURKEY AND QUINOA VEGGIE

PREP
20 MIN

COOK
30 MIN

DIFFICULTY
EASY

INGREDIENTS AND QUANTITIES

Ingredients	Puppy (<6 months)	Adult (>6 months-7 years)	Senior (7+ years)
Grilled turkey	100g / 3.5oz	150g / 5.3oz	120g / 4.2oz
Quinoa	40g / 1.4oz	80g / 2.8oz	60g / 2.1oz
Sweet potatoes	30g / 1oz	60g / 2.1oz	50g / 1.8oz
Green beans	30g / 1oz	60g / 2.1oz	50g / 1.8oz
Red bell peppers	20g / 0.7oz	40g / 1.4oz	30g / 1oz

METHOD

Grill Turkey: Grill the turkey until fully cooked, then chop it into small, bite-sized pieces.

Cook Quinoa: Prepare quinoa according to package instructions.

Steam Vegetables: Steam sweet potatoes, green beans, and red bell peppers until tender.

Combine Ingredients: In a bowl, mix together the grilled turkey, cooked quinoa, and steamed vegetables.

Serve: Let the meal cool to room temperature before serving to your dog.

ADVICE

- Ensure the turkey is thoroughly cooked to avoid any health risks.

- Cut all vegetables into small, manageable pieces for easier digestion.

- Adjust the portion sizes based on your dog's specific dietary requirements.

CHICKEN RICE AND VEGGIE MEDLEY

PREP
15 MIN

COOK
30 MIN

DIFFICULTY
EASY

INGREDIENTS AND QUANTITIES

Ingredients	Puppy (<6 months)	Adult (>6 months-7 years)	Senior (7+ years)
Baked chicken	100g / 3.5oz	150g / 5.3oz	120g / 4.2oz
Brown rice	50g / 1.8oz	100g / 3.5oz	80g / 2.8oz
Carrots	25g / 0.9oz	50g / 1.8oz	40g / 1.4oz
Peas	25g / 0.9oz	50g / 1.8oz	40g / 1.4oz
Spinach	20g / 0.7oz	40g / 1.4oz	30g / 1oz

METHOD

Bake Chicken: Bake the chicken in the oven until fully cooked, then chop it into small, bite-sized pieces.

Cook Rice: Prepare brown rice according to package instructions.

Steam Vegetables: Steam carrots, peas, and spinach until they are soft.

Combine Ingredients: Mix the baked chicken, cooked rice, and steamed vegetables in a bowl.

Serve: Let the meal cool to room temperature before serving.

ADVICE

- Ensure the chicken is fully cooked to prevent any health risks.

- Chop vegetables into small pieces to facilitate easy digestion.

- Adjust the quantity of food based on your dog's size, age, and activity level.

ROASTED DUCK AND BARLEY VEGGIE

PREP
25 MIN

COOK
40 MIN

DIFFICULTY
EASY

INGREDIENTS AND QUANTITIES

Ingredients	Puppy (<6 months)	Adult (>6 months-7 years)	Senior (7+ years)
Roasted duck	100g / 3.5oz	150g / 5.3oz	120g / 4.2oz
Barley	50g / 1.8oz	100g / 3.5oz	80g / 2.8oz
Butternut squash	30g / 1oz	60g / 2.1oz	50g / 1.8oz
Green peas	30g / 1oz	60g / 2.1oz	50g / 1.8oz
Kale	20g / 0.7oz	40g / 1.4oz	30g / 1oz

METHOD

Roast Duck: Roast the duck until it's tender, then shred it into small, bite-sized pieces.

Cook Barley: Prepare barley as per package instructions.

Steam Vegetables: Steam butternut squash, green peas, and kale until they are tender.

Combine Ingredients: In a bowl, mix the roasted duck, cooked barley, and steamed vegetables.

Serve: Cool the meal to room temperature before serving to your dog.

ADVICE

- Ensure the duck is thoroughly cooked to eliminate any health risks.

- Chop the vegetables into small, digestible pieces.

- Tailor the portion size to your dog's specific dietary requirements.

SALMON PASTA VEGGIE DELIGHT

PREP
20 MIN

COOK
30 MIN

DIFFICULTY
EASY

INGREDIENTS AND QUANTITIES

Ingredients	Puppy (<6 months)	Adult (>6 months-7 years)	Senior (7+ years)
Baked salmon	80g / 2.8oz	120g / 4.2oz	100g / 3.5oz
Whole grain pasta	40g / 1.4oz	80g / 2.8oz	60g / 2.1oz
Broccoli	20g / 0.7oz	40g / 1.4oz	30g / 1oz
Carrots	20g / 0.7oz	40g / 1.4oz	30g / 1oz
Tomatoes	20g / 0.7oz	40g / 1.4oz	30g / 1oz

METHOD

Bake Salmon: Bake the salmon until it's fully cooked, then flake it, ensuring no bones remain.

Cook Pasta: Prepare whole grain pasta according to package instructions.

Steam Vegetables: Steam broccoli, carrots, and tomatoes until they are tender.

Combine Ingredients: Mix the baked salmon, cooked pasta, and steamed vegetables in a bowl.

Serve: Allow the meal to cool to room temperature before serving to your dog.

ADVICE

- Ensure all bones are removed from the salmon to prevent choking hazards.

- Cut vegetables into small pieces for easier digestion.

- Adjust the portion size according to your dog's nutritional needs and size.

BEEF AND LENTIL VEGGIE MIX

PREP
20 MIN

COOK
35 MIN

DIFFICULTY
EASY

INGREDIENTS AND QUANTITIES

Ingredients	Puppy (<6 months)	Adult (>6 months-7 years)	Senior (7+ years)
Lean beef	100g / 3.5oz	150g / 5.3oz	120g / 4.2oz
Lentils	40g / 1.4oz	80g / 2.8oz	60g / 2.1oz
Pumpkin	30g / 1oz	60g / 2.1oz	50g / 1.8oz
Spinach	20g / 0.7oz	40g / 1.4oz	30g / 1oz
Cauliflower	30g / 1oz	60g / 2.1oz	50g / 1.8oz

METHOD

Cook Beef: Cook the lean beef in a pan until it's tender, then chop it into small pieces.

Boil Lentils: Prepare lentils according to package instructions.

Steam Vegetables: Steam the pumpkin, spinach, and cauliflower until they are tender.

Combine Ingredients: In a bowl, mix together the cooked beef, boiled lentils, and steamed vegetables.

Serve: Ensure the meal is cooled to room temperature before serving to your dog.

ADVICE

- Ensure the beef is thoroughly cooked to prevent any health risks.

- Chop the vegetables into small, digestible pieces.

- Balance the portion sizes based on your dog's age, size, and activity level.

CHICKEN AND RICE VEGETABLE

PREP
20 MIN

COOK
30 MIN

DIFFICULTY
EASY

INGREDIENTS AND QUANTITIES

Ingredients	Puppy (<6 months)	Adult (>6 months-7 years)	Senior (7+ years)
Grilled chicken	100g / 3.5oz	150g / 5.3oz	120g / 4.2oz
Brown rice	50g / 1.8oz	100g / 3.5oz	80g / 2.8oz
Carrots	25g / 0.9oz	50g / 1.8oz	40g / 1.4oz
Green beans	25g / 0.9oz	50g / 1.8oz	40g / 1.4oz
Sweet peas	25g / 0.9oz	50g / 1.8oz	40g / 1.4oz

METHOD

Grill Chicken: Grill the chicken until fully cooked, then chop it into small, bite-sized pieces.

Cook Rice: Prepare brown rice according to package instructions.

Steam Vegetables: Steam carrots, green beans, and sweet peas until they are tender.

Combine Ingredients: Mix the grilled chicken, cooked rice, and steamed vegetables in a bowl.

Serve: Let the meal cool to room temperature before serving to your dog.

ADVICE

- Ensure the chicken is thoroughly cooked to avoid any health risks.

- Cut the vegetables into small pieces to aid in digestion.

- Adjust the portion sizes to suit your dog's nutritional needs and size.

GRILLED PORK AND QUINOA VEGGIE

PREP
20 MIN

COOK
35 MIN

DIFFICULTY
EASY

INGREDIENTS AND QUANTITIES

Ingredients	Puppy (<6 months)	Adult (>6 months-7 years)	Senior (7+ years)
Grilled pork	100g / 3.5oz	150g / 5.3oz	120g / 4.2oz
Quinoa	40g / 1.4oz	80g / 2.8oz	60g / 2.1oz
Butternut squash	30g / 1oz	60g / 2.1oz	50g / 1.8oz
Kale	20g / 0.7oz	40g / 1.4oz	30g / 1oz
Red bell peppers	20g / 0.7oz	40g / 1.4oz	30g / 1oz

METHOD

Grill Pork: Grill the pork until fully cooked, then chop it into small, bite-sized pieces.

Cook Quinoa: Prepare quinoa according to package instructions.

Steam Vegetables: Steam butternut squash, kale, and red bell peppers until they are tender.

Combine Ingredients: In a bowl, mix together the grilled pork, cooked quinoa, and steamed vegetables.

Serve: Let the meal cool to room temperature before serving to your dog.

ADVICE

- Ensure the pork is thoroughly cooked to prevent any health risks.

- Chop vegetables into small pieces for easy digestion.

- Adjust the portion size based on your dog's size and nutritional needs.

TURKEY AND WHOLE WHEAT PASTA VEGGIE

PREP
20 MIN

COOK
40 MIN

DIFFICULTY
EASY

INGREDIENTS AND QUANTITIES

Ingredients	Puppy (<6 months)	Adult (>6 months-7 years)	Senior (7+ years)
Roasted turkey	100g / 3.5oz	150g / 5.3oz	120g / 4.2oz
Whole wheat pasta	40g / 1.4oz	80g / 2.8oz	60g / 2.1oz
Broccoli	25g / 0.9oz	50g / 1.8oz	40g / 1.4oz
Carrots	25g / 0.9oz	50g / 1.8oz	40g / 1.4oz
Sweet corn	25g / 0.9oz	50g / 1.8oz	40g / 1.4oz

METHOD

Roast Turkey: Roast the turkey until fully cooked, then shred it into small pieces.

Cook Pasta: Prepare whole wheat pasta according to package instructions.

Steam Vegetables: Steam broccoli, dice carrots, and cook sweet corn until they are tender.

Combine Ingredients: Mix the roasted turkey, cooked pasta, and steamed vegetables in a bowl.

Serve: Ensure the meal is at room temperature before serving it to your dog.

ADVICE

- Make sure the turkey is well cooked to avoid any health issues.

- Chop the vegetables into small, manageable pieces for easy digestion.

- Adjust portion sizes based on your dog's size, age, and activity level.

SLOW-COOKED BEEF AND OATMEAL VEGGIE

PREP
20 MIN

COOK
4/6 HOURS

DIFFICULTY
EASY

INGREDIENTS AND QUANTITIES

Ingredients	Puppy (<6 months)	Adult (>6 months-7 years)	Senior (7+ years)
Slow-cooked beef	100g / 3.5oz	150g / 5.3oz	120g / 4.2oz
Oatmeal	50g / 1.8oz	100g / 3.5oz	80g / 2.8oz
Pumpkin	30g / 1oz	60g / 2.1oz	50g / 1.8oz
Green beans	20g / 0.7oz	40g / 1.4oz	30g / 1oz
Beetroot	20g / 0.7oz	40g / 1.4oz	30g / 1oz

METHOD

Slow Cook Beef: Slow cook the beef until it's tender, then shred it into small pieces.

Cook Oatmeal: Prepare oatmeal according to package instructions.

Steam Vegetables: Steam the pumpkin and green beans, and boil the beetroot until tender.

Combine Ingredients: In a bowl, mix the slow-cooked beef, cooked oatmeal, and steamed vegetables.

Serve: Allow the meal to cool to room temperature before serving it to your dog.

ADVICE

- Ensure that the beef is cooked long enough to be easily digestible.

- Chop the vegetables into small pieces for easier eating and digestion.

- Adjust the portion sizes according to your dog's size, age, and dietary needs.

GRILLED LAMB AND BROWN RICE VEGGIE

PREP
20 MIN

COOK
30 MIN

DIFFICULTY
EASY

INGREDIENTS AND QUANTITIES

Ingredients	Puppy (<6 months)	Adult (>6 months-7 years)	Senior (7+ years)
Grilled lamb	100g / 3.5oz	150g / 5.3oz	120g / 4.2oz
Brown rice	50g / 1.8oz	100g / 3.5oz	80g / 2.8oz
Zucchini	30g / 1oz	60g / 2.1oz	50g / 1.8oz
Carrots	30g / 1oz	60g / 2.1oz	50g / 1.8oz
Peas	30g / 1oz	60g / 2.1oz	50g / 1.8oz

METHOD

Grill Lamb: Grill the lamb until it's fully cooked, then chop it into small, bite-sized pieces.

Cook Rice: Prepare brown rice according to package instructions.

Steam Vegetables: Steam zucchini, carrots, and peas until they are tender.

Combine Ingredients: In a bowl, mix the grilled lamb, cooked rice, and steamed vegetables.

Serve: Cool the meal to room temperature before serving to your dog.

ADVICE

- Make sure the lamb is thoroughly cooked to avoid any health risks.

- Chop the vegetables into small, manageable pieces for easier digestion.

- Balance the portion sizes according to your dog's nutritional needs and size.

BAKED FISH AND COUSCOUS VEGGIE

PREP
20 MIN

COOK
30 MIN

DIFFICULTY
EASY

INGREDIENTS AND QUANTITIES

Ingredients	Puppy (<6 months)	Adult (>6 months-7 years)	Senior (7+ years)
Baked fish	80g / 2.8oz	120g / 4.2oz	100g / 3.5oz
Couscous	40g / 1.4oz	80g / 2.8oz	60g / 2.1oz
Spinach	20g / 0.7oz	40g / 1.4oz	30g / 1oz
Sweet potatoes	30g / 1oz	60g / 2.1oz	50g / 1.8oz
Bell peppers	20g / 0.7oz	40g / 1.4oz	30g / 1oz

METHOD

Bake Fish: Bake the fish until it's flaky and ensure all bones are removed, then break it into small pieces.

Cook Couscous: Prepare couscous according to package instructions.

Steam Vegetables: Steam spinach, dice sweet potatoes, and chop bell peppers until tender.

Combine Ingredients: In a bowl, mix the baked fish, cooked couscous, and steamed vegetables.

Serve: Let the meal cool to room temperature before serving to your dog.

ADVICE

- Ensure all bones are removed from the fish to prevent choking hazards.

- Chop the vegetables into small, digestible pieces.

- Adjust portion sizes according to your dog's size and dietary needs.

ROASTED VENISON AND BARLEY VEGGIE

PREP
25 MIN

COOK
40 MIN

DIFFICULTY
EASY

INGREDIENTS AND QUANTITIES

Ingredients	Puppy (<6 months)	Adult (>6 months-7 years)	Senior (7+ years)
Roasted venison	100g / 3.5oz	150g / 5.3oz	120g / 4.2oz
Barley	40g / 1.4oz	80g / 2.8oz	60g / 2.1oz
Pumpkin	30g / 1oz	60g / 2.1oz	50g / 1.8oz
Kale	20g / 0.7oz	40g / 1.4oz	30g / 1oz
Beets	20g / 0.7oz	40g / 1.4oz	30g / 1oz

METHOD

Roast Venison: Roast the venison until it's tender, then chop it into small, bite-sized pieces.

Cook Barley: Prepare barley according to package instructions.

Steam Vegetables: Steam pumpkin, kale, and beets until they are tender.

Combine Ingredients: In a bowl, mix the roasted venison, cooked barley, and steamed vegetables.

Serve: Let the meal cool to room temperature before serving to your dog.

ADVICE

- Ensure the venison is thoroughly cooked to prevent any health risks.

- Chop the vegetables into small, manageable pieces for easier digestion.

- Adjust the portion sizes based on your dog's size and dietary needs..

LAMB AND SWEET POTATO VEGGIE

PREP
20 MIN

COOK
4/6 HOURS

DIFFICULTY
MODERATE

INGREDIENTS AND QUANTITIES

Ingredients	Puppy (<6 months)	Adult (>6 months-7 years)	Senior (7+ years)
Slow-cooked lamb	100g / 3.5oz	150g / 5.3oz	120g / 4.2oz
Sweet potatoes	50g / 1.8oz	100g / 3.5oz	80g / 2.8oz
Green beans	25g / 0.9oz	50g / 1.8oz	40g / 1.4oz
Carrots	25g / 0.9oz	50g / 1.8oz	40g / 1.4oz
Peas	25g / 0.9oz	50g / 1.8oz	40g / 1.4oz

METHOD

Slow Cook Lamb: Slow cook the lamb until it's tender, then shred it into small pieces.

Prepare Sweet Potatoes: Boil and mash the sweet potatoes.

Steam Vegetables: Steam green beans, dice carrots, and cook peas until tender.

Combine Ingredients: In a bowl, mix the slow-cooked lamb, mashed sweet potatoes, and steamed vegetables.

Serve: Allow the meal to cool to room temperature before serving to your dog.

ADVICE

- Ensure the lamb is cooked long enough to be easily digestible.

- Mash the sweet potatoes and chop the vegetables into small pieces for easier eating and digestion.

- Adjust the portion sizes based on your dog's size, age, and dietary needs.

GRILLED CHICKEN AND BROWN RICE

 **PREP**
20 MIN

 **COOK**
30 MIN

 **DIFFICULTY**
EASY

INGREDIENTS AND QUANTITIES

Ingredients	Puppy (<6 months)	Adult (>6 months-7 years)	Senior (7+ years)
Grilled chicken breast	100g / 3.5oz	150g / 5.3oz	120g / 4.2oz
Brown rice	50g / 1.8oz	100g / 3.5oz	80g / 2.8oz
Broccoli	25g / 0.9oz	50g / 1.8oz	40g / 1.4oz
Bell peppers	20g / 0.7oz	40g / 1.4oz	30g / 1oz

METHOD

Grill Chicken: Grill the chicken breast until fully cooked, then chop it into small, bite-sized pieces.

Cook Rice: Prepare brown rice according to package instructions.

Steam Vegetables: Steam broccoli, dice bell peppers, and slice carrots until tender.

Combine Ingredients: In a bowl, mix the grilled chicken, cooked rice, and steamed vegetables.

Serve: Ensure the meal is at room temperature before serving it to your dog.

ADVICE

- Make sure the chicken is thoroughly cooked to avoid any health risks.

- Chop the vegetables into small pieces for easier digestion.

- Adjust portion sizes based on your dog's size, age, and activity level.

GRILLED RABBIT AND MILLET VEGGIE

PREP
20 MIN

COOK
30 MIN

DIFFICULTY
MODERATE

INGREDIENTS AND QUANTITIES

Ingredients	Puppy (<6 months)	Adult (>6 months-7 years)	Senior (7+ years)
Grilled rabbit	100g / 3.5oz	150g / 5.3oz	120g / 4.2oz
Millet	40g / 1.4oz	80g / 2.8oz	60g / 2.1oz
Carrots	30g / 1oz	60g / 2.1oz	50g / 1.8oz
Zucchini	30g / 1oz	60g / 2.1oz	50g / 1.8oz
Peas	25g / 0.9oz	50g / 1.8oz	40g / 1.4oz

METHOD

Grill Rabbit: Grill the rabbit until it's fully cooked, then chop it into small, bite-sized pieces.

Cook Millet: Prepare millet according to package instructions.

Steam Vegetables: Steam carrots, slice zucchini, and cook peas until tender.

Combine Ingredients: In a bowl, mix the grilled rabbit, cooked millet, and steamed vegetables.

Serve: Cool the meal to room temperature before serving to your dog.

ADVICE

- Ensure the rabbit is thoroughly cooked to prevent any health risks.

- Chop the vegetables into small, manageable pieces for easier digestion.

- Adjust the portion sizes based on your dog's size and nutritional needs.

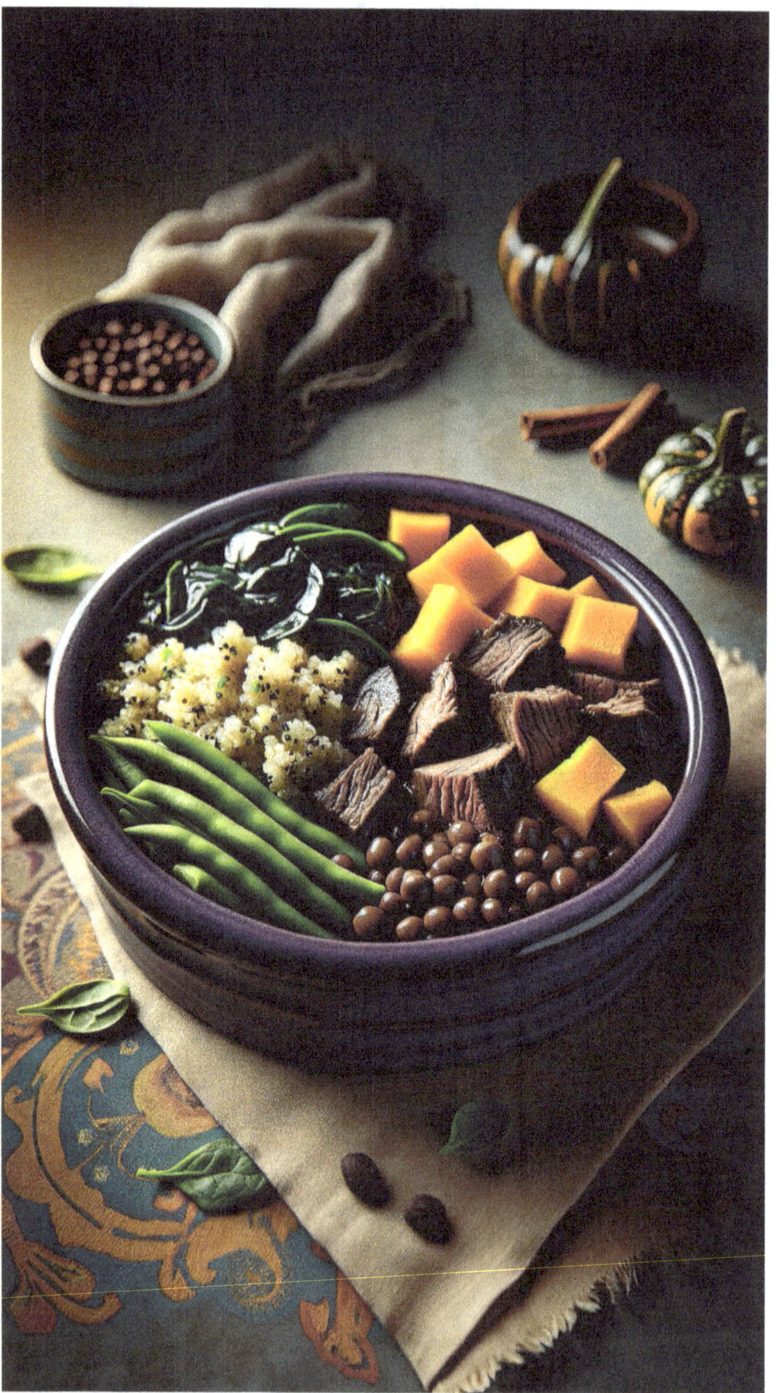

BRAISED BEEF AND QUINOA VEGGIE

PREP
20 MIN

COOK
3/3 HOURS

DIFFICULTY
MODERATE

INGREDIENTS AND QUANTITIES

Ingredients	Puppy (<6 months)	Adult (>6 months-7 years)	Senior (7+ years)
Braised beef	100g / 3.5oz	150g / 5.3oz	120g / 4.2oz
Quinoa	40g / 1.4oz	80g / 2.8oz	60g / 2.1oz
Butternut squash	30g / 1oz	60g / 2.1oz	50g / 1.8oz
Green beans	25g / 0.9oz	50g / 1.8oz	40g / 1.4oz
Spinach	20g / 0.7oz	40g / 1.4oz	30g / 1oz

METHOD

Braise Beef: Braise the beef until it's tender, then chop it into small, bite-sized pieces.

Cook Quinoa: Prepare quinoa according to package instructions.

Steam Vegetables: Steam butternut squash, green beans, and spinach until they are tender.

Combine Ingredients: In a bowl, mix the braised beef, cooked quinoa, and steamed vegetables.

Serve: Let the meal cool to room temperature before serving to your dog.

ADVICE

- Ensure the beef is tender and easy to digest.

- Chop the vegetables into small pieces for easier eating and digestion.

- Adjust the portion sizes according to your dog's size, age, and dietary needs.

DOG BISCUITS

PEANUT BUTTER & PUMPKIN

PREP
15 MIN

COOK
40 MIN

DIFFICULTY
EASY

INGREDIENTS AND QUANTITIES

Ingredients	Puppy (<6 months)	Adult (>6 months-7 years)	Senior (7+ years)
Whole wheat flour	1 cup / 120g	2 cups / 240g	1 ½ cups / 180g
Pumpkin puree (unsweetened)	¼ cup / 60g	½ cup / 120g	½ cup / 80g
Natural peanut butter (no xylitol)	2 tbsp / 30g	3 tbsp / 45g	2 ½ tbsp / 37g
Eggs	1	2	1
Water (if needed)	1-2 tbsp / 15-30ml	2-3 tbsp / 30-45ml	1-2 tbsp / 15-30ml

METHOD

Preheat Oven: Set your oven to 350°F (175°C).

Combine Dry Ingredients: In a large bowl, mix together the whole wheat flour.

Add Wet Ingredients: Stir in the pumpkin puree, peanut butter, and eggs. Mix until a dough forms. If it's too dry, add a little water.

Roll Out Dough: On a floured surface, roll out the dough to about ¼ inch thickness.

Cut Out Biscuits: Use a cookie cutter to cut out shapes from the dough.

Bake: Place the biscuits on a baking sheet and bake for 35-40 minutes or until hard.

Cool Down: Let the biscuits cool completely before serving to your dog.

ADVICE

- Ensure the peanut butter is free from xylitol and other artificial sweeteners.

- You can store these biscuits in an airtight container for up to a week, or freeze them for longer storage.

- Always supervise your dog when giving them any new treat.

SIMPLE OAT AND APPLE

PREP
10 MIN

COOK
25 MIN

DIFFICULTY
EASY

INGREDIENTS AND QUANTITIES

Ingredients	Puppy (<6 months)	Adult (>6 months-7 years)	Senior (7+ years)
Rolled oats	1 cup / 80g	2 cups / 160g	1 ½ cups / 120g
Unsweetened applesauce	¼ cup / 60ml	½ cup / 120ml	1/3 cup / 80ml
Whole wheat flour	½ cup / 60g	1 cup / 120g	¾ cup / 90g
Water	2 tbsp / 30ml	¼ cup / 60ml	3 tbsp / 45ml

METHOD

Preheat Oven: Set your oven to 350°F (175°C).

Mix Ingredients: In a large bowl, combine the oats, applesauce, whole wheat flour, and water. Stir until a dough forms.

Roll and Cut: Roll the dough out on a floured surface to about ¼ inch thick. Use cookie cutters to cut into shapes.

Bake: Place the biscuits on a baking sheet and bake for 20-25 minutes or until they are golden brown.

Cool Down: Allow the biscuits to cool completely before serving.

ADVICE

- Always use unsweetened applesauce to avoid excess sugar.

- Store the biscuits in an airtight container for up to a week or freeze for longer storage.

- Monitor your dog's reaction to new treats, especially if they have sensitive stomachs.

CHICKEN & CARROT

PREP
15 MIN

COOK
30 MIN

DIFFICULTY
EASY

INGREDIENTS AND QUANTITIES

Ingredients	Puppy (<6 months)	Adult (>6 months-7 years)	Senior (7+ years)
Boiled chicken, shredded	½ cup / 65g	1 cup / 130g	¾ cup / 100g
Grated carrots	¼ cup / 30g	½ cup / 60g	1/3 cup / 40g
Whole wheat flour	1 cup / 120g	2 cups / 240g	1 ½ cups / 180g
Low-sodiu chicken broth	¼ cup / 60ml	½ cup / 120ml	1/3 cup / 80ml
Egg	1	2	1

METHOD

Preheat Oven: Set your oven to 350°F (175°C).

Combine Ingredients: In a bowl, mix together the shredded chicken, grated carrots, whole wheat flour, chicken broth, and egg until well combined.

Form Biscuits: Roll out the dough on a floured surface and use a cookie cutter to cut into shapes.

Bake: Place the biscuits on a lined baking sheet and bake for 25-30 minutes or until crispy.

Cool Down: Let the biscuits cool completely before giving them to your dog.

ADVICE

- Ensure the chicken is cooked without any added spices or seasonings.

- Carrots are a great low-calorie snack for dogs, rich in vitamins.

- Store these biscuits in an airtight container for up to a week, or freeze them for longer storage.

SWEET POTATO & APPLE

PREP
15 MIN

COOK
35 HOURS

DIFFICULTY
EASY

INGREDIENTS AND QUANTITIES

Ingredients	Puppy (<6 months)	Adult (>6 months-7 years)	Senior (7+ years)
Cooked sweet potato, mashed	½ cup / 115g	1 cup / 230g	¾ cup / 172g
Finely chopped apple (skin removed)	¼ cup / 30g	½ cup / 60g	1/3 cup / 40g
Whole wheat flour	1 cup / 120g	2 cups / 240g	1 ½ cups / 180g
Egg	1	2	1
Water (if needed)	1-2 tbsp / 15-30ml	2-3 tbsp / 30-45ml	1-2 tbsp / 15-30ml

METHOD

Preheat Oven: Set your oven to 350°F (175°C).

Combine Ingredients: In a large bowl, mix the mashed sweet potato, chopped apple, whole wheat flour, and egg. Add a little water if the dough is too dry.

Roll Out Dough: On a floured surface, roll out the dough to about ¼ inch thick.

Cut Shapes: Use cookie cutters to cut the dough into desired shapes.

Bake: Place the biscuits on a baking sheet and bake for 30-35 minutes until they turn golden brown.

Cool: Allow the biscuits to cool completely before serving.

ADVICE

- Make sure the apple is finely chopped and skin removed to avoid any choking hazard.

- Sweet potatoes are a great source of vitamins but should be given in moderation.

- These biscuits can be stored in an airtight container for up to a week orfrozen for longer storage.

BEEF & PARSLEY

PREP
20 MIN

COOK
30 MIN

DIFFICULTY
EASY

INGREDIENTS AND QUANTITIES

Ingredients	Puppy (<6 months)	Adult (>6 months-7 years)	Senior (7+ years)
Cooked lean beef, minced	½ cup / 115g	1 cup / 230g	¾ cup / 172g
Chopped fresh parsley	2 tbsp / 7.5g	¼ cup / 15g	3 tbsp / 11g
Whole wheat flour	1 cup / 120g	2 cups / 240g	1 ½ cups / 180g
Low-sodium beef broth	¼ cup / 60ml	½ cup / 120ml	1/3 cup / 80ml
Egg	1	50g / 1.8oz	1

METHOD

Preheat Oven: Set your oven to 350°F (175°C).

Mix Ingredients: In a large bowl, combine the minced beef, chopped parsley, whole wheat flour, beef broth, and egg.

Form the Dough: Mix well until a dough forms. If it's too dry, add a little more broth.

Roll and Cut: Roll out the dough on a floured surface and use cookie cutters to cut into shapes.

Bake: Place the biscuits on a baking sheet and bake for 25-30 minutes until they turn golden and crispy.

Cool Down: Let the biscuits cool completely before serving to your dog.

ADVICE

- Ensure the beef is cooked without any spices or seasonings.

- Parsley can help freshen a dog's breath but should be used in moderation.

- Store these biscuits in an airtight container for up to a week, or freeze them for longer storage.

TURKEY AND VEGETABLE

PREP
20 MIN

COOK
25 MIN

DIFFICULTY
EASY

INGREDIENTS AND QUANTITIES

Ingredients	Puppy (<6 months)	Adult (>6 months-7 years)	Senior (7+ years)
Cooked ground turkey	½ cup / 115g	1 cup / 230g	¾ cup / 172g
Pureed pumpkin (unsweetened)	¼ cup / 60g	½ cup / 120g	1/3 cup / 80g
Finely chopped spinach	¼ cup / 60g	½ cup /120g	1/3 cup / 80g
Whole wheat flour	1 cup / 120g	2 cups / 240g	1 ½ cups / 180g
Egg	1	2	1

METHOD

Preheat Oven: Set your oven to 350°F (175°C).

Combine Ingredients: In a large bowl, mix together the cooked turkey, pumpkin puree, chopped spinach, whole wheat flour, and egg.

Form Dough: Stir well until a dough forms.

Roll Out Dough: On a floured surface, roll the dough to about ¼ inch thickness.

Cut Out Biscuits: Use cookie cutters to cut the dough into desired shapes.

Bake: Place the biscuits on a lined baking sheet and bake for 25-30 minutes until golden brown.

Cool: Allow the biscuits to cool completely before serving.

ADVICE

- Ensure the turkey is cooked thoroughly without any added spices or seasonings.

- Spinach is a good source of vitamins but should be given in moderation.

- These biscuits can be stored in an airtight container for up to a week, or frozen for longer storage.

FISH & SWEET PEA

PREP
15 MIN

COOK
20 MIN

DIFFICULTY
EASY

INGREDIENTS AND QUANTITIES

Ingredients	Puppy (<6 months)	Adult (>6 months-7 years)	Senior (7+ years)
Cooked and flaked fish (e.g., salmon or cod)	½ cup / 115g	1 cup / 230g	¾ cup / 172g
Pureed sweet peas	¼ cup / 60g	½ cup / 120g	1/3 cup / 80g
Whole wheat flour	1 cup / 120g	2 cups / 240g	1 ½ cups / 180g
Egg	1	2	1

METHOD

Preheat Oven: Set your oven to 350°F (175°C).

Mix Ingredients: In a large bowl, combine the cooked fish, sweet pea puree, whole wheat flour, and egg.

Create Dough: Stir until a dough forms. If it's too dry, add a little water.

Roll and Cut: On a floured surface, roll the dough out and use cookie cutters to cut into shapes.

Bake: Place the biscuits on a baking sheet and bake for 20-25 minutes or until golden brown.

Cool: Let the biscuits cool completely before serving.

ADVICE

- Ensure the fish is cooked thoroughly and free of bones.

- Sweet peas are a good source of vitamins and fiber but should be given in moderation.

- Store the biscuits in an airtight container for up to a week or freeze for longer storage.

BANANA & BLUEBERRY

PREP
15 MIN

COOK
25 MIN

DIFFICULTY
EASY

INGREDIENTS AND QUANTITIES

Ingredients	Puppy (<6 months)	Adult (>6 months-7 years)	Senior (7+ years)
Mashed ripe banana	1/3cup / 75g	2/3 cup / 150g	½ cup / 115g
Fresh blueberries	¼ cup / 35g	½ cup / 70g	1/3 cup / 50g
Whole wheat flour	1 cup / 120g	2 cups / 240g	1 ½ cups / 180g
Egg	1	2	1
Water (if needed)	1-2 tbsp / 15-30ml	2-3 tbsp / 30-45ml	1-2 tbsp / 15-30ml

METHOD

Preheat Oven: Set your oven to 350°F (175°C).

Blend Ingredients: In a bowl, mix the mashed banana, blueberries, whole wheat flour, and egg. Add water if the mixture is too dry.

Form Dough: Knead the mixture until it forms a dough.

Roll and Cut: Roll the dough on a floured surface and use cookie cutters to cut into shapes.

Bake: Place the biscuits on a baking sheet and bake for 20-25 minutes until golden.

Cool: Allow the biscuits to cool completely before serving to your dog.

ADVICE

- Use ripe bananas for natural sweetness and easier digestion.

- Blueberries are a great source of antioxidants but should be given in moderation.

- These biscuits can be stored in an airtight container for up to a week or frozen for extended freshness.

PEANUT BUTTER & HONEY

PREP
10 MIN

COOK
20 MIN

DIFFICULTY
EASY

INGREDIENTS AND QUANTITIES

Ingredients	Puppy (<6 months)	Adult (>6 months-7 years)	Senior (7+ years)
Natural peanut butter (no xylitol)	¼ cup / 60g	½ cup / 120g	1/3 cup / 80g
Honey	1 tbsp / 15ml	2 tbsp / 30ml	1 ½ tbsp / 22ml
Whole wheat flour	1 ½ cups / 180g	3 cups / 360g	2 ¼ cups / 270g
Egg	1	2	1
Water	2 tbsp / 30ml	¼ cup / 60ml	3 tbsp / 45ml

METHOD

Preheat Oven: Set your oven to 350°F (175°C).

Mix Ingredients: In a large bowl, combine peanut butter, honey, whole wheat flour, egg, and water.

Form Dough: Stir well until a dough forms. Add a bit more water if it's too dry.

Roll Out Dough: On a floured surface, roll the dough to about ¼ inch thick.

Cut Biscuits: Use cookie cutters to cut the dough into desired shapes.

Bake: Place the biscuits on a baking sheet and bake for 18-20 minutes or until golden brown.

Cool: Allow the biscuits to cool completely before serving to your dog.

ADVICE

- Ensure the peanut butter is free from xylitol and other artificial sweeteners.

- Honey can add a touch of natural sweetness but should be used in moderation.

- Store these biscuits in an airtight container for up to a week, or freeze them for longer storage.

CRANBERRY & OAT

PREP
15 MIN

COOK
25 HOURS

DIFFICULTY
EASY

INGREDIENTS AND QUANTITIES

Ingredients	Puppy (<6 months)	Adult (>6 months-7 years)	Senior (7+ years)
Dried cranberries, unsweetened	¼ cup / 30g	½ cup / 60g	1/3 cup / 40g
Rolled oats	1 cup / 80g	2 cups / 160g	1 ½ cups / 120g
Whole wheat flour	1 cup / 120g	2 cups / 240g	1 ½ cups / 180g
Egg	1	2	1
Water	2-3 tbsp / 30-45ml	¼ cup / 60ml	3 tbsp / 45ml

METHOD

Preheat Oven: Set the oven to 350°F (175°C).

Combine Ingredients: In a large bowl, mix together the dried cranberries, oats, whole wheat flour, egg, and water.

Form Dough: Stir until a cohesive dough forms.

Roll and Cut: On a floured surface, roll out the dough to ¼ inch thickness and use cookie cutters to cut into shapes.

Bake: Arrange the biscuits on a baking sheet and bake for 20-25 minutes or until golden.

Cool: Let the biscuits cool completely before offering them to your dog.

ADVICE

- Make sure to use unsweetened dried cranberries to avoid excess sugar.

- Oats are a good source of fiber and can be gentle on a dog's stomach.

- These biscuits can be stored in an airtight container for up to a week, or frozen for extended freshness.

CHICKEN & RICE

PREP
15 MIN

COOK
20 MIN

DIFFICULTY
EASY

INGREDIENTS AND QUANTITIES

Ingredients	Puppy (<6 months)	Adult (>6 months-7 years)	Senior (7+ years)
Cooked chicken, finely chopped	½ cup / 65g	1 cup / 130g	¾ cup / 100g
Cooked rice	½ cup / 90g	1 cup / 180g	¾ cup / 135g
Whole wheat flour	1 cup / 120g	2 cups / 240g	1 ½ cups / 180g
Low-sodium chicken broth	¼ cup / 60ml	½ cup / 120ml	1/3 cup / 80ml
Egg	1	2	1

METHOD

Preheat Oven: Set your oven to 350°F (175°C).

Mix Ingredients: In a large bowl, combine the chicken, rice, whole wheat flour, chicken broth, and egg.

Form Dough: Stir well until a dough forms. If it's too dry, add a little more broth.

Roll and Cut: Roll out the dough on a floured surface and use cookie cutters to cut into shapes.

Bake: Place the biscuits on a baking sheet and bake for 20-25 minutes until they turn golden brown.

Cool: Let the biscuits cool completely before serving.

ADVICE

- Ensure the chicken is cooked thoroughly and without any added spices or seasonings.

- Rice can be a good source of energy for dogs but should be given in moderation.

- These biscuits can be stored in an airtight container for up to a week, or frozen for longer storage.

CHEESY SPINACH

PREP
20 MIN

COOK
25 MIN

DIFFICULTY
EAY

INGREDIENTS AND QUANTITIES

Ingredients	Puppy (<6 months)	Adult (>6 months-7 years)	Senior (7+ years)
Shredded low-fat cheese	¼ cup / 30g	½ cup / 60g	1/3 cup / 40g
Chopped fresh spinach	¼ cup / 30g	½ cup / 60g	1/3 cup / 40g
Whole wheat flour	1 ½ cups / 180g	3 cups / 360g	2 ¼ cups / 270g
Low-sodium chicken broth	¼ cup / 60ml	½ cup / 120ml	1/3 cup / 80ml
Egg	1	2	1

METHOD

Preheat Oven: Set your oven to 350°F (175°C).

Combine Ingredients: In a large bowl, mix the shredded cheese, spinach, whole wheat flour, chicken broth, and egg.

Knead Dough: Work the mixture into a dough. If it's too dry, add a bit more broth.

Roll and Cut: Roll out the dough on a floured surface and use cookie cutters to cut into shapes.

Bake: Place the biscuits on a baking sheet and bake for 25 minutes or until crispy.

Cool: Let the biscuits cool completely before giving them to your dog.

ADVICE

- Use low-fat cheese to avoid excessive fat intake.

- Spinach is a great source of vitamins and iron but should be given in moderation.

- These biscuits can be stored in an airtight container for up to a week or frozen for longer storage.

PUMPKIN & FLAXSEED

PREP
15 MIN

COOK
30 MIN

DIFFICULTY
EASY

INGREDIENTS AND QUANTITIES

Ingredients	Puppy (<6 months)	Adult (>6 months-7 years)	Senior (7+ years)
Pumpkin puree (unsweetened)	1/3 cup / 80g	2/3 cup / 160g	½ cup / 120g
Ground flaxseed	2 tbsp / 14g	3 tbsp / 21g	2 ½ tbsp / 17.5g
Whole wheat flour	1 ½ cups / 180g	3 cups / 360g	2 ¼ cups / 270g
Water	2 tbsp / 30ml	¼ cup / 60ml	3 tbsp / 45ml
Egg	1	2	1

METHOD

Preheat Oven: Set your oven to 350°F (175°C).

Mix Ingredients: In a large bowl, blend the pumpkin puree, ground flaxseed, whole wheat flour, water, and egg.

Form Dough: Stir until a dough forms. Add a bit more water if necessary.

Roll and Cut: Roll out the dough on a floured surface and use cookie cutters to cut into shapes.

Bake: Arrange the biscuits on a baking sheet and bake for 30 minutes or until they are golden brown.

Cool: Let the biscuits cool completely before serving.

ADVICE

- Pumpkin is a great source of fiber and can aid in digestive health.

- Flaxseed is rich in omega-3 fatty acids, which are good for a dog's coat and skin.

- Store these biscuits in an airtight container for up to a week, or freeze them for extended freshness.

BEETROOT & APPLE

PREP
15 MIN

COOK
25 HOURS

DIFFICULTY
EASY

INGREDIENTS AND QUANTITIES

Ingredients	Puppy (<6 months)	Adult (>6 months-7 years)	Senior (7+ years)
Pureed beetroot	¼ cup / 60g	½ cup / 120g	1/3 cup / 80g
Grated apple (skin removed)	¼ cup / 30g	½ cup / 60g	1/3 cup / 40g
Whole wheat flour	1 cup / 120g	2 cups / 240g	1 ½ cups / 180g
Egg	1	2	1

METHOD

Preheat Oven: Set your oven to 350°F (175°C).

Combine Ingredients: In a large bowl, mix together the beetroot puree, grated apple, whole wheat flour, and egg.

Form Dough: Stir until a dough forms.

Roll and Cut: On a floured surface, roll the dough to about ¼ inch thickness and use cookie cutters to cut into shapes.

Bake: Place the biscuits on a baking sheet and bake for 25-30 minutes until they turn golden brown.

Cool: Allow the biscuits to cool completely before serving.

ADVICE

- Choose unsweetened beetroot puree to avoid added sugars.

- Ensure the apple is finely grated and skin removed for easy digestion.

- These biscuits can be stored in an airtight container for up to a week or frozen for longer storage.

COCONUT & CAROB

PREP
15 MIN

COOK
20 MIN

DIFFICULTY
EASY

INGREDIENTS AND QUANTITIES

Ingredients	Puppy (<6 months)	Adult (>6 months-7 years)	Senior (7+ years)
Unsweetened shredded coconut	¼ cup / 20g	½ cup / 40g	1/3 cup / 30g
Carob powder	2 tbsp / 10g	3 tbsp / 15g	2 ½ tbsp / 12.5g
Whole wheat flour	1 cup / 120g	2 cups / 240g	1 ½ cups / 180g
Egg	1	2	1
Water	2-3 tbsp / 30-45ml	¼ cup / 60ml	3 tbsp / 45ml

METHOD

Preheat Oven: Set the oven to 350°F (175°C).

Mix Ingredients: In a large bowl, combine the shredded coconut, carob powder, whole wheat flour, egg, and water.

Form Dough: Stir until a dough forms.

Roll and Cut: Roll out the dough on a floured surface to about ¼ inch thick and use cookie cutters to cut into shapes.

Bake: Place the biscuits on a baking sheet and bake for 20-25 minutes until they turn golden brown.

Cool: Let the biscuits cool completely before serving.

ADVICE

- Ensure the coconut is unsweetened to avoid added sugars.

- Carob is a dog-safe alternative to chocolate and can be used to add flavor.

- Store the biscuits in an airtight container for up to a week or freeze for longer shelf life.

LIVER & PARSLEY

PREP
20 MIN

COOK
25 MIN

DIFFICULTY
EASY

INGREDIENTS AND QUANTITIES

Ingredients	Puppy (<6 months)	Adult (>6 months-7 years)	Senior (7+ years)
Cooked and minced liver (beef or chicken)	½ cup / 115g	1 cup / 230g	¾ cup / 172g
Chopped fresh parsley	2 tbsp / 7.5g	¼ cup / 15g	3 tbsp / 11g
Whole wheat flour	1 cup / 120g	2 cups / 240g	1 ½ cups / 180g
Low-sodium beef or chicken broth	¼ cup / 60ml	½ cup / 120ml	1/3 cup / 80ml
Egg	1	2	1

METHOD

Preheat Oven: Set your oven to 350°F (175°C).

Combine Ingredients: In a large bowl, mix the minced liver, parsley, whole wheat flour, broth, and egg.

Form Dough: Knead until a dough forms. Add a bit more broth if too dry.

Roll and Cut: Roll out the dough on a floured surface and use cookie cutters to cut into shapes.

Bake: Place the biscuits on a baking sheet and bake for 25 minutes or until they turn golden brown.

Cool: Allow the biscuits to cool completely before serving to your dog.

ADVICE

- Ensure the liver is cooked thoroughly without any added spices or seasonings.

- Parsley can help freshen a dog's breath and is also a good source of vitamins.

- Store the biscuits in an airtight container for up to a week, or freeze them for longer storage.

APPLE & CINNAMON

PREP
20 MIN

COOK
30 MIN

DIFFICULTY
EASY

INGREDIENTS AND QUANTITIES

Ingredients	Puppy (<6 months)	Adult (>6 months-7 years)	Senior (7+ years)
Finely chopped apple (skin removed)	½ cup / 60g	1 cup / 120g	¾ cup / 90g
Ground cinnamon	1 tsp / 2.6g	2 tsp / 5.2g	1 ½ tsp / 3.9g
Whole wheat flour	1 ½ cups / 180g	3 cups / 360g	2 ¼ cups / 270g
Water	¼ cup / 60ml	½ cup / 120ml	1/3 cup / 80ml
Egg	1	2	1

METHOD

Preheat Oven: Set your oven to 350°F (175°C).

Combine Ingredients: In a large bowl, mix the chopped apple, cinnamon, whole wheat flour, water, and egg.

Form Dough: Knead until a dough forms.

Roll and Cut: Roll out the dough on a floured surface and use cookie cutters to cut into shapes.

Bake: Place the biscuits on a baking sheet and bake for 25-30 minutes until they turn golden brown.

Cool: Allow the biscuits to cool completely before serving.

ADVICE

- Make sure the apple is finely chopped to avoid any choking hazard.

- Cinnamon can add flavor and is generally safe for dogs in small quantities.

- These biscuits can be stored in an airtight container for up to a week or frozen for longer storage.

PEANUT BUTTER & BANANA

PREP
15 MIN

COOK
20 MIN

DIFFICULTY
EASY

INGREDIENTS AND QUANTITIES

Ingredients	Puppy (<6 months)	Adult (>6 months-7 years)	Senior (7+ years)
Natural peanut butter (no xylitol)	¼ cup / 60g	½ cup / 120g	1/3 cup / 80g
Mashed ripe banana	1/3 cup / 75g	2/3 cup / 150g	½ cup / 115g
Whole wheat flour	1 cup / 120g	2 cups / 240g	1 ½ cups / 180g
Egg	1	2	1

METHOD

Preheat Oven: Set the oven to 350°F (175°C).

Mix Ingredients: In a large bowl, combine the peanut butter, mashed banana, whole wheat flour, and egg.

Form Dough: Stir until a dough forms.

Roll and Cut: Roll out the dough on a floured surface to about ¼ inch thick, and use cookie cutters to cut into shapes.

Bake: Place the biscuits on a baking sheet and bake for 20-25 minutes until golden brown.

Cool: Let the biscuits cool completely before serving.

ADVICE

- Ensure the peanut butter is free from xylitol and other artificial sweeteners.

- Bananas are a great source of potassium and fiber but should be given in moderation.

- These biscuits can be stored in an airtight container for up to a week or frozen for longer storage.

CARROT & ZUCCHINI

PREP
20 MIN

COOK
30 MIN

DIFFICULTY
EASY

INGREDIENTS AND QUANTITIES

Ingredients	Puppy (<6 months)	Adult (>6 months-7 years)	Senior (7+ years)
Grated carrot	½ cup / 60g	1 cup / 120g	¾ cup / 90g
Grated zucchini	½ cup / 60g	1 cup / 120g	¾ cup / 90g
Whole wheat flour	1 ½ cups / 180g	3 cups / 360g	2 ¼ cups / 270g
Low-sodium vegetable broth	¼ cup / 60ml	½ cup / 120ml	1/3 cup / 80ml
Egg	1	2	1

METHOD

Preheat Oven: Set your oven to 350°F (175°C).

Combine Ingredients: In a large bowl, mix the grated carrot, zucchini, whole wheat flour, vegetable broth, and egg.

Form Dough: Stir until a dough forms. Add more broth if needed.

Roll and Cut: Roll out the dough on a floured surface and use cookie cutters to cut into shapes.

Bake: Place the biscuits on a baking sheet and bake for 25-30 minutes until they are golden brown.

Cool: Allow the biscuits to cool completely before serving.

ADVICE

- Carrots and zucchini are great sources of vitamins and fiber.

- Ensure the broth is low in sodium and free of onions or garlic.

- These biscuits can be stored in an airtight container for up to a week or frozen for longer storage.

SWEET POTATO & CHIA SEED

PREP
20 MIN

COOK
30 MIN

DIFFICULTY
EASY

INGREDIENTS AND QUANTITIES

Ingredients	Puppy (<6 months)	Adult (>6 months-7 years)	Senior (7+ years)
Cooked swee potato, mashed	½ cup / 115g	1 cup / 230g	¾ cup / 172g
Chia seeds	1 tbsp / 10g	2 tbsp / 20g	1 ½ tbsp / 15g
Whole wheat flour	1 ½ cups / 180g	3 cups / 360g	2 ¼ cups / 270g
Water	¼ cup / 60ml	½ cup / 120ml	1/3 cup / 80ml
Egg	1	2	1

METHOD

Preheat Oven: Set your oven to 350°F (175°C).

Mix Ingredients: In a large bowl, combine the mashed sweet potato, chia seeds, whole wheat flour, water, and egg.

Form Dough: Stir until a dough forms.

Roll and Cut: Roll out the dough on a floured surface to about ¼ inch thick, and use cookie cutters to cut into shapes.

Bake: Place the biscuits on a baking sheet and bake for 30 minutes until they are golden brown.

Cool: Let the biscuits cool completely before serving.

ADVICE

- Sweet potatoes are a great source of vitamins and fiber.

- Chia seeds are rich in omega-3 fatty acids, which can be beneficial for a dog's coat and skin health.

- Store these biscuits in an airtight container for up to a week or freeze for longer shelf life.

PEANUT BUTTER & OATS

PREP
15 MIN

COOK
20 MIN

DIFFICULTY
EASY

INGREDIENTS AND QUANTITIES

Ingredients	Puppy (<6 months)	Adult (>6 months-7 years)	Senior (7+ years)
Natural peanut butter (no xylitol)	1/3 cup / 80g	2/3 cup / 160g	½ cup / 120g
Rolled oats	1 cup / 80g	2 cups / 160g	1 ½ cups / 120g
Whole wheat flour	1 cup / 120g	2 cups / 240g	1 ½ cups / 180g
Water	¼ cup / 60ml	½ cup / 120ml	1/3 cup / 80ml
Egg	1	2	1

METHOD

Preheat Oven: Set the oven to 350°F (175°C).

Mix Ingredients: In a large bowl, combine the peanut butter, oats, whole wheat flour, water, and egg.

Form Dough: Stir until a dough forms.

Roll and Cut: Roll out the dough on a floured surface to about ¼ inch thick, and use cookie cutters to cut into shapes.

Bake: Place the biscuits on a baking sheet and bake for 20-25 minutes until golden brown.

Cool: Let the biscuits cool completely before serving.

ADVICE

- Ensure the peanut butter is free from xylitol and other artificial sweeteners.

- Oats are a good source of fiber and can be gentle on a dog's digestive system.

- Store these biscuits in an airtight container for up to a week or freeze for - longer shelf life.

BLUEBERRY & YOGURT

PREP
15 MIN

COOK
20 MIN

DIFFICULTY
EASY

INGREDIENTS AND QUANTITIES

Ingredients	Puppy (<6 months)	Adult (>6 months-7 years)	Senior (7+ years)
Fresh blueberries	¼ cup / 35g	½ cup / 70g	1/3 cup / 50g
Plain, unsweetened yogurt	¼ cup / 60g	½ cup / 120g	1/3 cup / 80g
Whole wheat flour	1 cup / 120g	2 cups / 240g	1 ½ cups / 180g
Egg	1	2	1

METHOD

Preheat Oven: Set your oven to 350°F (175°C).

Mix Ingredients: In a large bowl, combine the blueberries, yogurt, whole wheat flour, and egg.

Form Dough: Stir until a dough forms. If it's too dry, add a bit more yogurt.

Roll and Cut: Roll out the dough on a floured surface and use cookie cutters to cut into shapes.

Bake: Place the biscuits on a baking sheet and bake for 20 minutes until they are golden brown.

Cool: Let the biscuits cool completely before serving.

ADVICE

- Use plain, unsweetened yogurt to avoid added sugars and artificial sweeteners.

- Blueberries are a great source of antioxidants but should be given in moderation.

- These biscuits can be stored in an airtight container for up to a week or frozen for longer shelf life.

CHICKEN & RICE 2

PREP
20 MIN

COOK
30 MIN

DIFFICULTY
EASY

INGREDIENTS AND QUANTITIES

Ingredients	Puppy (<6 months)	Adult (>6 months-7 years)	Senior (7+ years)
Cooked chicken, minced	½ cup / 115g	1 cup / 230g	¾ cup / 172g
Cooked rice	½ cup / 90g	1 cup / 180g	¾ cup / 135g
Whole wheat flour	1 cup / 120g	2 cups / 240g	1 ½ cups / 180g
Low-sodium chicken broth	¼ cup / 60ml	½ cup / 120ml	1/3 cup / 80ml
Egg	1	2	1

METHOD

Preheat Oven: Set your oven to 350°F (175°C).

Combine Ingredients: In a large bowl, mix the cooked chicken, rice, whole wheat flour, chicken broth, and egg.

Form Dough: Stir until a dough forms. If too dry, add more broth.

Roll and Cut: On a floured surface, roll out the dough and use cookie cutters to cut into shapes.

Bake: Place the biscuits on a baking sheet and bake for 25-30 minutes until they turn golden brown.

Cool: Let the biscuits cool completely before serving to your dog.

ADVICE

- Ensure the chicken is cooked thoroughly and without spices or seasonings.

- Rice is a good source of energy for dogs but should be given in moderation.

- Store the biscuits in an airtight container for up to a week, or freeze for longer shelf life.

BEEF & BROCCOLI

PREP
20 MIN

COOK
30 MIN

DIFFICULTY
EASY

INGREDIENTS AND QUANTITIES

Ingredients	Puppy (<6 months)	Adult (>6 months-7 years)	Senior (7+ years)
Cooked ground beef	½ cup / 115g	1 cup / 230g	¾ cup / 172g
Finely chopped broccoli	¼ cup / 30g	½ cup / 60g	1/3 cup / 40g
Whole wheat flour	1 ½ cups / 180g	3 cups / 360g	2 ¼ cups / 270g
Low-sodium beef broth	¼ cup / 60ml	½ cup / 120ml	1/3 cup / 80ml
Egg	1	2	1

METHOD

Preheat Oven: Set your oven to 350°F (175°C).

Combine Ingredients: In a large bowl, mix the cooked ground beef, broccoli, whole wheat flour, beef broth, and egg.

Form Dough: Stir until a dough forms. If it's too dry, add more broth.

Roll and Cut: Roll out the dough on a floured surface and use cookie cutters to cut into shapes.

Bake: Place the biscuits on a baking sheet and bake for 30 minutes until they turn golden brown.

Cool: Let the biscuits cool completely before serving.

ADVICE

- Ensure the beef is cooked thoroughly and without any spices or seasonings.

- Broccoli is a good source of vitamins but should be given in ù moderation due to its potentially gassy nature.

- Store these biscuits in an airtight container for up to a week, or freeze for longer storage.

TURKEY & CRANBERRY

PREP
20 MIN

COOK
30 MIN

DIFFICULTY
EASY

INGREDIENTS AND QUANTITIES

Ingredients	Puppy (<6 months)	Adult (>6 months-7 years)	Senior (7+ years)
Cooked ground turkey	½ cup / 115g	1 cup / 230g	¾ cup / 172g
Dried cranberries, unsweetened	¼ cup / 30g	½ cup / 60g	1/3 cup / 40g
Whole wheat flour	1 ½ cups / 180g	3 cups / 360g	2 ¼ cups / 270g
Low-sodium chicken broth	¼ cup / 60ml	½ cup / 120ml	1/3 cup / 80ml
Egg	1	2	1

METHOD

Preheat Oven: Set your oven to 350°F (175°C).

Combine Ingredients: In a large bowl, mix the cooked turkey, cranberries, whole wheat flour, chicken broth, and egg.

Form Dough: Stir until a dough forms. Add more broth if needed.

Roll and Cut: Roll out the dough on a floured surface and use cookie cutters to cut into shapes.

Bake: Place the biscuits on a baking sheet and bake for 30 minutes until they turn golden brown.

Cool: Let the biscuits cool completely before serving to your dog.

ADVICE

- Ensure the turkey is cooked thoroughly and without any spices or seasonings.

- Use unsweetened dried cranberries to avoid added sugars.

- Store these biscuits in an airtight container for up to a week, or freeze for longer shelf life.

DOG CAKES

PEANUT BUTTER AND APPLE

PREP
15 MIN

COOK
30 MIN

DIFFICULTY
EASY

INGREDIENTS AND QUANTITIES

Ingredients	Puppy (<6 months)	Adult (>6 months-7 years)	Senior (7+ years)
Whole wheat flour	75g / 2.6oz	150g / 5.3oz	120g / 4.2oz
Baking powder	1g / 0.03oz	2g / 0.07oz	1.5g / 0.05oz
Egg	1 (small)	1 (medium)	1 (small)
Unsweetened apple sauce	30g / 1oz	60g / 2.1oz	50g / 1.8oz
Natural peanu butter (no xylitol)	30g / 1oz	60g / 2.1oz	50g / 1.8oz
Finely chopped apple (peeled)	40g / 1.4oz	80g / 2.8oz	65g / 2.3oz
Carrot (grated)	20g / 0.7oz	40g / 1.4oz	30g / 1.1oz
Water	30ml / 1oz	60ml / 2oz	50ml / 1.7oz

METHOD

Preheat the oven to 180°C (350°F).

In a bowl, mix together the whole wheat flour and baking powder.

In a separate bowl, beat the egg and then mix in the unsweetened apple sauce, natural peanut butter, finely chopped apple, and grated carrot.

Gradually add the dry ingredients to the wet ingredients, mixing well. Add water as needed to get a batter consistency.

Pour the batter into a greased cake pan.

Bake for 30 minutes or until a toothpick inserted in the center comes out clean.

Let the cake cool before serving to your dog.

ADVICE

- Ensure all peanut butter used does not contain xylitol.

- Always peel the apple to avoid any potential harmful effects from the skin.

- You can top the cake with a light spread of peanut butter or plain yogurt for an extra treat.

BANANA AND CARROT

PREP
20 MIN

COOK
30 MIN

DIFFICULTY
EASY

INGREDIENTS AND QUANTITIES

Ingredients	Puppy (<6 months)	Adult (>6 months-7 years)	Senior (7+ years)
Whole wheat flour	80g / 2.8oz	160g / 5.6oz	130g / 4.6oz
Baking soda	1g / 0.03oz	2g / 0.07oz	1.5g / 0.05oz
Mashed ripe banana	50g / 1.8oz	100g / 3.5oz	80g / 2.8oz
Grated carrot	30g / 1oz	60g / 2.1oz	50g / 1.8oz
Natural peanut butter (no xylitol)	25g / 0.9oz	50g / 1.8oz	40g / 1.4oz
Egg	1 (small)	1 (medium)	1 (small)
Water	20ml / 0.7oz	40ml / 1.4oz	30ml / 1oz

METHOD

Preheat the oven to 175°C (350°F).

In a bowl, combine the whole wheat flour and baking soda.

In another bowl, mix the mashed banana, grated carrot, natural peanut butter, and egg.

Gradually add the dry ingredients to the wet mixture, adding water as needed to achieve a cake batter consistency.

Pour the mixture into a greased cake pan.

Bake for 40 minutes or until a toothpick inserted in the center comes out clean.

Allow the cake to cool before serving.

ADVICE

- Use ripe bananas for a natural sweetness.

- Make sure the peanut butter is free from xylitol and other harmful additives.

- Grate the carrot finely to ensure it cooks thoroughly and is easy for your dog to digest.

BLUEBERRY AND OATMEAL

PREP
20 MIN

COOK
25 MIN

DIFFICULTY
EASY

INGREDIENTS AND QUANTITIES

Ingredients	Puppy (<6 months)	Adult (>6 months-7 years)	Senior (7+ years)
Rolled oats	50g / 1.8oz	100g / 3.5oz	80g / 2.8oz
Whole wheat flour	60g / 2.1oz	120g / 4.2oz	90g / 3.2oz
Baking powder	1g / 0.03oz	2g / 0.07oz	1.5g / 0.05oz
Mashed banana	40g / 1.4oz	80g / 2.8oz	60g / 2.1oz
Fresh blueberries	30g / 1oz	60g / 2.1oz	45g / 1.6oz
Unsweetened applesauce	25g / 0.9oz	50g / 1.8oz	40g / 1.4oz
Egg	1 (small)	1 (medium)	1 (small)
Water	15ml / 0.5oz	30ml / 1oz	25ml / 0.9oz

METHOD

Preheat the oven to 180°C (350°F).

Blend the rolled oats in a food processor until they reach a flour-like consistency.

In a bowl, mix the oat flour, whole wheat flour, and baking powder.

In another bowl, combine the mashed banana, fresh blueberries, unsweetened applesauce, and egg.

Slowly mix the dry ingredients into the wet mixture, adding water to achieve a smooth batter.

Spoon the batter into a greased muffin tin or small cake pan.

Bake for 25 minutes or until a toothpick comes out clean.

Allow the cakes to cool before serving to your dog.

ADVICE

- Choose fresh, organic blueberries for the best flavor and health benefits.

- Ensure the oats are pure and free from added sugars or flavors.

- This cake can be stored in an airtight container in the fridge for up to 5 days.

PUMPKIN AND YOGURT

PREP
20 MIN

COOK
35 MIN

DIFFICULTY
EASY

INGREDIENTS AND QUANTITIES

Ingredients	Puppy (<6 months)	Adult (>6 months-7 years)	Senior (7+ years)
Whole wheat flour	85g / 3oz	170g / 6oz	135g / 4.8oz
Baking powder	1g / 0.03oz	2g / 0.07oz	1.5g / 0.05oz
Canned pumpkin (pure, no spices)	60g / 2.1oz	120g / 4.2oz	95g / 3.4oz
Natural plain yogurt (low-fat)	30g / 1oz	60g / 2.1oz	45g / 1.6oz
Egg	1 (small)	1 (medium)	1 (small)
Honey	10g / 0.35oz	20g / 0.7oz	15g / 0.5oz
Carrot (grated)	25g / 0.9oz	50g / 1.8oz	40g / 1.4oz
Water	20ml / 0.7oz	40ml / 1.4oz	30ml / 1oz

METHOD

Preheat the oven to 180°C (350°F).

Mix the whole wheat flour and baking powder in a bowl.

In a separate bowl, blend the canned pumpkin, natural yogurt, egg, and honey.

Gradually add the dry ingredients to the wet mixture, combining well. Stir in the grated carrot. Add water as necessary for a cake batter consistency.

Pour the batter into a greased cake pan.

Bake for 35 minutes or until a toothpick inserted comes out clean.

Cool the cake before serving.

ADVICE

- Ensure the pumpkin is pure and does not contain added sugars or spices.

- Choose low-fat, natural yogurt to keep it healthier for your dog.

- The honey can be omitted if you prefer a less sweet cake.

SWEET POTATO AND CHICKEN

PREP
25 MIN

COOK
45 MIN

DIFFICULTY
MODERATE

INGREDIENTS AND QUANTITIES

Ingredients	Puppy (<6 months)	Adult (>6 months-7 years)	Senior (7+ years)
Cooked, mashed sweet potato	100g / 3.5oz	200g / 7oz	150g / 5.3oz
Ground chicken, cooked	75g / 2.6oz	150g / 5.3oz	120g / 4.2oz
Whole wheat flour	90g / 3.2oz	180g / 6.3oz	140g / 4.9oz
Eggs	2 (small)	2 (medium)	2 (small)
Carrot, grated	40g / 1.4oz	80g / 2.8oz	60g / 2.1oz
Plain Greek yogurt (low-fat)	30g / 1oz	60g / 2.1oz	45g / 1.6oz
Water	25ml / 0.8oz	50ml / 1.7oz	40ml / 1.4oz

METHOD

Preheat the oven to 180°C (350°F).

In a large bowl, combine the cooked, mashed sweet potato, ground chicken, and grated carrot.

Stir in the whole wheat flour.

Beat the eggs and mix them into the batter. Add water to adjust the consistency.

Pour the mixture into a greased baking pan.

Bake for 45 minutes, or until the cake is firm and cooked through.

Let it cool, then top with a spread of plain Greek yogurt before serving.Allow the cakes to cool before serving to your dog.

ADVICE

- Ensure the chicken is thoroughly cooked and cooled before adding to the mix.

- The Greek yogurt topping can be omitted or replaced with a dog-friendly frosting.

- Sweet potato is a great source of vitamins but should be given in moderation.

BEEF AND PEA POOCH

PREP
30 MIN

COOK
50 MIN

DIFFICULTY
MODERATE

INGREDIENTS AND QUANTITIES

Ingredients	Puppy (<6 months)	Adult (>6 months-7 years)	Senior (7+ years)
Ground beef, cooked	100g / 3.5oz	200g / 7oz	150g / 5.3oz
Green peas, cooked	50g / 1.8oz	100g / 3.5oz	75g / 2.6oz
Whole wheat flour	95g / 3.4oz	190g / 6.7oz	145g / 5.1oz
Egg	2 (small)	2 (medium)	2 (small)
Carrot, grated	45g / 1.6oz	90g / 3.2oz	70g / 2.5oz
Olive oil	5ml / 0.17oz	10ml / 0.34oz	8ml / 0.27oz
Water	30ml / 1oz	60ml / 2oz	45ml / 1.5oz

METHOD

Preheat the oven to 175°C (350°F).

In a large bowl, mix the cooked ground beef, cooked green peas, and grated carrot.

Stir in the whole wheat flour.

Whisk the eggs and olive oil together, then blend into the meat and vegetable mixture. Add water to reach a moist but firm consistency.

Transfer the mixture into a greased pie or cake pan.

Bake for 50 minutes, or until the top is golden brown and the pie is cooked through.

Allow to cool before serving.

ADVICE

- Make sure the beef is lean and thoroughly cooked to avoid any health issues.

- Peas are a good source of vitamins but should be used in moderation.

- This pie can be stored in the refrigerator for up to 4 days.

TURKEY AND SPINACH PUP LOAF

PREP
20 MIN

COOK
40 MIN

DIFFICULTY
EASY

INGREDIENTS AND QUANTITIES

Ingredients	Puppy (<6 months)	Adult (>6 months-7 years)	Senior (7+ years)
Ground turkey, cooked	120g / 4.2oz	240g / 8.5oz	180g / 6.3oz
Chopped spinach, cooked	40g / 1.4oz	80g / 2.8oz	60g / 2.1oz
Whole wheat flour	100g / 3.5oz	200g / 7oz	150g / 5.3oz
Eggs	2 (small)	2 (medium)	2 (small)
Carrot, grated	50g / 1.8oz	100g / 3.5oz	75g / 2.6oz
Unsweetened applesauce	30g / 1oz	60g / 2.1oz	45g / 1.6oz
Water	35ml / 1.2oz	70ml / 2.4oz	55ml / 1.9oz

METHOD

Preheat the oven to 180°C (350°F).

In a large bowl, mix together the cooked ground turkey and chopped spinach.

Add the whole wheat flour, grated carrot, and unsweetened applesauce to the mixture.

Beat the eggs and stir them into the bowl, then gradually add water to achieve a loaf-like consistency.

Transfer the mixture into a greased loaf pan.

Bake for 40 minutes or until the loaf is firm and cooked through.

Cool before slicing and serving to your dog.

ADVICE

- Use lean turkey to keep it healthier for your dog.

- Ensure the spinach is plain and free from any added spices or oils.

- This loaf can be refrigerated for up to 5 days and is great for slicing as needed.

SALMON AND ZUCCHINI

PREP
20 MIN

COOK
35 MIN

DIFFICULTY
EASY

INGREDIENTS AND QUANTITIES

Ingredients	Puppy (<6 months)	Adult (>6 months-7 years)	Senior (7+ years)
Canned salmon, drained	85g / 3oz	170g / 6oz	130g / 4.6oz
Grated zucchini	60g / 2.1oz	120g / 4.2oz	90g / 3.2oz
Whole wheat flour	75g / 2.6oz	150g / 5.3oz	115g / 4oz
Egg	1 (small)	2 (medium)	1 (small)
Olive oil	5ml / 0.17oz	10ml / 0.34oz	8ml / 0.27oz
Parsley, finely chopped	5g / 0.2oz	10g / 0.35oz	8g / 0.28oz
Water	20ml / 0.7oz	40ml / 1.4oz	30ml / 1oz

METHOD

Preheat the oven to 175°C (350°F).

In a bowl, mix the drained salmon and grated zucchini.

Add the whole wheat flour and chopped parsley to the salmon mixture.

Beat the egg with olive oil and blend into the mixture, adding water as needed to create a batter.

Spoon the batter into a greased muffin tin or small cake pan.

Bake for 35 minutes, or until the cakes are golden and firm.

Allow to cool before serving to your dog.

ADVICE

- Choose boneless, skinless canned salmon for ease and safety.

- Zucchini should be fresh and finely grated.

- Parsley can freshen your dog's breath but use it in moderation.

APPLE AND OAT POOCH

PREP
15 MIN

COOK
30 MIN

DIFFICULTY
EASY

INGREDIENTS AND QUANTITIES

Ingredients	Puppy (<6 months)	Adult (>6 months-7 years)	Senior (7+ years)
Rolled oats	60g / 2.1oz	120g / 4.2oz	90g / 3.2oz
Whole wheat flour	70g / 2.5oz	140g / 4.9oz	105g / 3.7oz
Baking powder	1g / 0.03oz	2g / 0.07oz	1.5g / 0.05oz
Egg	1 (small)	1 (medium)	1 (small)
Unsweetened applesauce	40g / 1.4oz	80g / 2.8oz	60g / 2.1oz
Peeled, finely diced apple	50g / 1.8oz	100g / 3.5oz	75g / 2.6oz
Water	25ml / 0.8oz	50ml / 1.7oz	40ml / 1.4oz

METHOD

Preheat the oven to 180°C (350°F).

Blend the rolled oats in a food processor until they reach a flour-like consistency.

Mix the oat flour, whole wheat flour, and baking powder in a bowl.

In another bowl, beat the egg and mix in the unsweetened applesauce and finely diced apple.

Gradually add the dry ingredients to the wet mixture, adding water to achieve a batter consistency.

Pour the batter into a greased cake pan.

Bake for 30 minutes or until a toothpick inserted comes out clean.

Let the cake cool before serving to your dog.

ADVICE

- Choose a sweet variety of apple for a natural, dog-friendly sweetness.

- Ensure the apple is peeled and finely diced to prevent any choking hazards.

- This cake can be kept in the refrigerator for up to 5 days.

CHICKEN AND BROCCOLI

PREP
20 MIN

COOK
30 MIN

DIFFICULTY
EASY

INGREDIENTS AND QUANTITIES

Ingredients	Puppy (<6 months)	Adult (>6 months-7 years)	Senior (7+ years)
Ground chicken, cooked	100g / 3.5oz	200g / 7oz	150g / 5.3oz
Chopped broccoli, cooked	50g / 1.8oz	100g / 3.5oz	75g / 2.6oz
Brown rice flour	80g / 2.8oz	160g / 5.6oz	120g / 4.2oz
Egg	1 (small)	2 (medium)	1 (small)
Olive oil	5ml / 0.17oz	10ml / 0.34oz	8ml / 0.27oz
Low-fat cottage cheese	30g / 1oz	60g / 2.1oz	45g / 1.6oz
Water	30ml / 1oz	60ml / 2oz	45ml / 1.5oz

METHOD

Preheat the oven to 180°C (350°F).

In a bowl, mix the cooked ground chicken and chopped broccoli.

Stir in the brown rice flour.

Whisk together the egg and olive oil, then mix into the chicken and broccoli. Add water to reach a batter-like consistency.

Spoon the batter into a greased muffin tin or small cake pan.

Bake for 30 minutes or until the cakes are firm and golden.

Let them cool before topping with a dollop of low-fat cottage cheese.

ADVICE

- Ensure the broccoli is cooked and chopped finely to make it easier for your dog to digest.

- Brown rice flour is a good gluten-free option that's gentle on a dog's stomach.

- Cottage cheese adds a tasty and calcium-rich topping, but use it sparingly if your dog is lactose intolerant.

BEET AND CARROT

PREP
15 MIN

COOK
25 MIN

DIFFICULTY
EASY

INGREDIENTS AND QUANTITIES

Ingredients	Puppy (<6 months)	Adult (>6 months-7 years)	Senior (7+ years)
Cooked beet, pureed	50g / 1.8oz	100g / 3.5oz	75g / 2.6oz
Grated carrot	40g / 1.4oz	80g / 2.8oz	60g / 2.1oz
Whole wheat flour	70g / 2.5oz	140g / 4.9oz	110g / 3.9oz
Egg	1 (small)	1 (medium)	1 (small)
Unsweetened applesauce	30g / 1oz	60g / 2.1oz	45g / 1.6oz
Water	20ml / 0.7oz	40ml / 1.4oz	30ml / 1oz

METHOD

Preheat the oven to 180°C (350°F).

In a bowl, combine the pureed beet and grated carrot.

Stir in the whole wheat flour.

Beat the egg and mix it with the unsweetened applesauce. Blend this into the beet and carrot mixture, adding water as needed to form a smooth batter.

Spoon the batter into a greased muffin tin.

Bake for 25 minutes or until the cupcakes are firm and a toothpick comes out clean.

Allow to cool before serving to your dog.

ADVICE

- Be sure to use plain cooked beets without any added salt or spices.

- Carrots add a natural sweetness and are great for your dog's teeth.

- These cupcakes can be stored in the refrigerator for up to 5 days.

BANANA AND BLUEBERRY

PREP
15 MIN

COOK
30 MIN

DIFFICULTY
EASY

INGREDIENTS AND QUANTITIES

Ingredients	Puppy (<6 months)	Adult (>6 months-7 years)	Senior (7+ years)
Mashed ripe banana	60g / 2.1oz	120g / 4.2oz	90g / 3.2oz
Fresh blueberries	40g / 1.4oz	80g / 2.8oz	60g / 2.1oz
Whole wheat flour	75g / 2.6oz	150g / 5.3oz	115g / 4oz
Egg	1 (small)	1 (medium)	1 (small)
Natural yogurt (low-fat)	30g / 1oz	60g / 2.1oz	45g / 1.6oz
Water	25ml / 0.8oz	50ml / 1.7oz	40ml / 1.4oz

METHOD

Preheat the oven to 180°C (350°F).

In a bowl, mix the mashed banana with the fresh blueberries.

Stir in the whole wheat flour.

Beat the egg and blend it into the mixture. Add the natural yogurt, mixing thoroughly. Add water to achieve a batter consistency.

Pour the batter into a greased cake pan.

Bake for 30 minutes or until a toothpick inserted comes out clean.

Let the cake cool before serving to your dog.

ADVICE

- Choose ripe bananas for natural sweetness and easy digestion.

- Ensure the yogurt is plain and low in fat, avoiding any artificial sweeteners.

- Blueberries are great antioxidants but use them in moderation.

PEANUT BUTTER AND PUMPKIN

PREP
20 MIN

COOK
35 MIN

DIFFICULTY
EASY

INGREDIENTS AND QUANTITIES

Ingredients	Puppy (<6 months)	Adult (>6 months-7 years)	Senior (7+ years)
Whole wheat flour	80g / 2.8oz	160g / 5.6oz	120g / 4.2oz
Baking powder	1g / 0.03oz	2g / 0.07oz	1.5g / 0.05oz
Canned pumpkin (pure, no spices)	70g / 2.5oz	140g / 4.9oz	105g / 3.7oz
Natural peanut butter (no xylitol)	40g / 1.4oz	80g / 2.8oz	60g / 2.1oz
Egg	1 (small)	1 (medum)	1 (small)
Water	30ml / 1oz	60ml / 2oz	45ml / 1.5oz

METHOD

Preheat the oven to 175°C (350°F).

In a bowl, mix the whole wheat flour and baking powder.

Add the canned pumpkin and natural peanut butter to the dry ingredients.

Beat the egg and blend it into the mixture. Gradually add water to achieve a smooth, cake-like batter.

Pour the batter into a greased cake pan.

Bake for 35 minutes or until a toothpick inserted comes out clean.

Allow the cake to cool before serving to your dog.

ADVICE

- Ensure the peanut butter is xylitol-free and doesn't contain artificial sweeteners.

- Use pure canned pumpkin, not the pie filling which may contain added sugars and spices.

- This cake can be stored in the refrigerator for up to 4 days.

CHICKEN AND SWEET POTATO

PREP
25 MIN

COOK
40 MIN

DIFFICULTY
MODERATE

INGREDIENTS AND QUANTITIES

Ingredients	Puppy (<6 months)	Adult (>6 months-7 years)	Senior (7+ years)
Cooked, mashed sweet potato	85g / 3oz	170g / 6oz	130g / 4.6oz
Ground chicken, cooked	75g / 2.6oz	150g / 5.3oz	120g / 4.2oz
Whole wheat flour	90g / 3.2oz	180g / 6.3oz	140g / 4.9oz
Egg	2 (small)	2 (medium)	2 (small)
Grated carrot	50g / 1.8oz	100g / 3.5oz	80g / 2.8oz
Unsweetened applesauce	35g / 1.2oz	70g / 2.5oz	55g / 1.9oz
Water	30ml / 1oz	60ml / 2oz	50ml / 1.7oz

METHOD

Preheat the oven to 180°C (350°F).

In a large bowl, mix together the mashed sweet potato and cooked ground chicken.

Add the whole wheat flour, grated carrot, and unsweetened applesauce to the mixture.

Beat the eggs and mix them into the batter. Add water to adjust the consistency.

Pour the mixture into a greased cake pan.

Bake for 40 minutes, or until the cake is firm and cooked through.

Let it cool, then serve to your dog.

ADVICE

- Ensure the sweet potato is cooked until soft and mashed thoroughly.

- Use lean ground chicken to keep the cake healthier.

- This cake can be refrigerated and served over several days.

TURKEY AND GREEN BEAN

PREP
25 MIN

COOK
50 MIN

DIFFICULTY
MODERATE

INGREDIENTS AND QUANTITIES

Ingredients	Puppy (<6 months)	Adult (>6 months-7 years)	Senior (7+ years)
Ground turkey, cooked	120g / 4.2oz	240g / 8.5oz	180g / 6.3oz
Chopped green beans, cooked	60g / 2.1oz	120g / 4.2oz	90g / 3.2oz
Whole wheat flour	100g / 3.5oz	200g / 7oz	150g / 5.3oz
Egg	2 (small)	2 (medium)	2 (small)
Carrot, grated	70g / 2.5oz	140g / 4.9oz	105g / 3.7oz
Unsweetened applesauce	40g / 1.4oz	80g / 2.8oz	60g / 2.1oz
Water	35ml / 1.2oz	70ml / 2.4oz	55ml / 1.9oz

METHOD

Preheat the oven to 180°C (350°F).

In a large bowl, combine the cooked ground turkey and chopped green beans.

Stir in the whole wheat flour and grated carrot.

Beat the eggs and mix them with the unsweetened applesauce. Gradually blend this into the turkey mixture, adding water to achieve a pie-like consistency.

Transfer the mixture into a greased pie or cake pan.

Bake for 50 minutes, or until the pie is golden brown and cooked through.

Allow to cool before serving.

ADVICE

- Use lean turkey to make the pie healthier for your dog.

- Ensure the green beans are plain and free from any added spices or oils.

- This pie can be stored in the refrigerator for up to 4 days.

LAMB AND MINT

PREP
20 MIN

COOK
35 MIN

DIFFICULTY
MODERATE

INGREDIENTS AND QUANTITIES

Ingredients	Puppy (<6 months)	Adult (>6 months-7 years)	Senior (7+ years)
Ground lamb, cooked	90g / 3.2oz	180g / 6.3oz	135g / 4.8oz
Fresh mint, finely chopped	5g / 0.2oz	10g / 0.35oz	8g / 0.28oz
Whole wheat flour	75g / 2.6oz	150g / 5.3oz	115g / 4oz
Egg	1 (small)	2 (medium)	1 (small)
Carrot, grated	40g / 1.4oz	80g / 2.8oz	60g / 2.1oz
Unsweetened applesauce	25g / 0.9oz	50g / 1.8oz	40g / 1.4oz
Water	20ml / 0.7oz	40ml / 1.4oz	30ml / 1oz

METHOD

Preheat the oven to 180°C (350°F).

In a bowl, mix the cooked ground lamb and finely chopped fresh mint.

Add the whole wheat flour and grated carrot to the lamb mixture.

Beat the egg and mix it with the unsweetened applesauce. Blend into the mixture, adding water to achieve a batter-like consistency.

Spoon the batter into a greased muffin tin or small cake pan.

Bake for 35 minutes, or until the pupcakes are firm and golden.

Cool before serving to your dog.

ADVICE

- Ensure the lamb is lean and cooked thoroughly to avoid any health issues.

- Fresh mint can help freshen your dog's breath but use it in moderation.

- These pupcakes can be stored in the refrigerator for up to 4 days.

FISH AND PARSLEY

PREP
20 MIN

COOK
35 MIN

DIFFICULTY
EASY

INGREDIENTS AND QUANTITIES

Ingredients	Puppy (<6 months)	Adult (>6 months-7 years)	Senior (7+ years)
Canned tuna or salmon, drained	100g / 3.5oz	200g / 7oz	150g / 5.3oz
Finely chopped parsley	10g / 0.35oz	20g / 0.7oz	15g / 0.5oz
Whole wheat flour	90g / 3.2oz	180g / 6.3oz	135g / 4.8oz
Egg	1 (small)	2 (medium)	1 (small)
Carrot, grated	60g / 2.1oz	120g / 4.2oz	90g / 3.2oz
Olive oil	10ml / 0.34oz	20ml / 0.68oz	15ml / 0.5oz
Water	30ml / 1oz	60ml / 2oz	45ml / 1.5oz

METHOD

Preheat the oven to 175°C (350°F).

In a bowl, mix together the drained tuna or salmon and finely chopped parsley.

Add the whole wheat flour and grated carrot.

Beat the egg and olive oil together, then mix into the fish mixture. Gradually add water to form a consistent batter.

Pour the batter into a greased cake pan.

Bake for 35 minutes or until the cake is firm and golden.

Cool before serving to your dog.

ADVICE

- Choose canned fish in water, not oil, and ensure it's free from added salt or spices.

- Parsley is great for freshening breath but use it in moderation.

- This cake can be refrigerated for up to 4 days.

BEEF AND BROWN RICE

PREP
25 MIN

COOK
45 MIN

DIFFICULTY
MODERATE

INGREDIENTS AND QUANTITIES

Ingredients	Puppy (<6 months)	Adult (>6 months-7 years)	Senior (7+ years)
Ground beef, cooked	120g / 4.2oz	240g / 8.5oz	180g / 6.3oz
Cooked brown rice	70g / 2.5oz	140g / 4.9oz	105g / 3.7oz
Whole wheat flour	80g / 2.8oz	160g / 5.6oz	120g / 4.2oz
Egg	2 (small)	2 (medium)	2 (small)
Grated carrot	50g / 1.8oz	100g / 3.5oz	75g / 2.6oz
Chopped parsley	10g / 0.35oz	20g / 0.7oz	15g / 0.5oz
Water	30ml / 1oz	60ml / 2oz	45ml / 1.5oz

METHOD

Preheat the oven to 180°C (350°F).

In a large bowl, combine the cooked ground beef, cooked brown rice, and grated carrot.

Stir in the whole wheat flour and chopped parsley.

Beat the eggs and add them to the bowl, mixing thoroughly. Gradually add water to achieve a loaf consistency.

Transfer the mixture into a greased loaf pan.

Bake for 45 minutes or until the loaf is firm and golden brown.

Cool before slicing and serving to your dog.

ADVICE

- Ensure the ground beef is lean and thoroughly cooked.

- Brown rice provides a healthy source of fiber but should be given in moderation.

- This loaf can be refrigerated and served over several days.

APPLE CINNAMON

PREP
20 MIN

COOK
30 MIN

DIFFICULTY
EASY

INGREDIENTS AND QUANTITIES

Ingredients	Puppy (<6 months)	Adult (>6 months-7 years)	Senior (7+ years)
Whole wheat flour	85g / 3oz	170g / 6oz	130g / 4.6oz
Unsweetened applesauce	45g / 1.6oz	90g / 3.2oz	70g / 2.5oz
Finely chopped apple	50g / 1.8oz	100g / 3.5oz	75g / 2.6oz
Ground cinnamon	1g / 0.03oz	2g / 0.07oz	1.5g / 0.05oz
Egg	1 (small)	1 (medium)	1 (small)
Vegetable oil	5ml / 0.17oz	10ml / 0.34oz	8ml / 0.27oz
Water	30ml / 1oz	60ml / 2oz	45ml / 1.5oz

METHOD

Preheat the oven to 175°C (350°F).

In a bowl, combine the whole wheat flour and ground cinnamon.

Stir in the unsweetened applesauce and finely chopped apple.

Beat the egg with vegetable oil and mix into the batter. Add water to achieve a cake-like consistency.

Pour the mixture into a greased cake pan.

Bake for 30 minutes or until a toothpick inserted in the center comes out clean.

Let the cake cool before serving to your dog.

ADVICE

- Choose a sweet variety of apple for natural flavor.

- Ensure the cinnamon is used in moderation as it's just for flavor.

- This cake can be stored in the refrigerator for up to 5 days.

PEANUT BUTTER AND BANANA

PREP
15 MIN

COOK
25 MIN

DIFFICULTY
MODERATE

INGREDIENTS AND QUANTITIES

Ingredients	Puppy (<6 months)	Adult (>6 months-7 years)	Senior (7+ years)
Whole wheat flour	70g / 2.5oz	140g / 4.9oz	110g / 3.9oz
Natural peanut butter (no xylitol)	30g / 1oz	60g / 2.1oz	45g / 1.6oz
Mashed ripe banana	50g / 1.8oz	100g / 3.5oz	75g / 2.6oz
Egg	1 (small)	1 (medium)	1 (small)
Water	20ml / 0.7oz	40ml / 1.4oz	30ml / 1oz

METHOD

Preheat the oven to 180°C (350°F).

In a bowl, mix the whole wheat flour.

Add the natural peanut butter and mashed banana, mixing until well combined.

Beat in the egg and add water to achieve a thick batter consistency.

Spoon the batter into a greased muffin tin or small cake pan.

Bake for 25 minutes or until a toothpick inserted comes out clean.

Cool before serving to your dog.

ADVICE

- Ensure the peanut butter does not contain xylitol or any other harmful additives.

- Ripe bananas are best for natural sweetness and easier digestion.

- These cupcakes can be stored in the refrigerator for up to 4 days.

CARROT AND APPLE

PREP
15 MIN

COOK
20 MIN

DIFFICULTY
EASY

INGREDIENTS AND QUANTITIES

Ingredients	Puppy (<6 months)	Adult (>6 months-7 years)	Senior (7+ years)
Whole wheat flour	60g / 2.1oz	120g / 4.2oz	90g / 3.2oz
Grated carrot	40g / 1.4oz	80g / 2.8oz	60g / 2.1oz
Finely diced apple	40g / 1.4oz	80g / 2.8oz	60g / 2.1oz
Unsweetened applesauce	30g / 1oz	60g / 2.1oz	45g / 1.6oz
Egg	1 (small)	1 (medium)	1 (small)
Water	20ml / 0.7oz	40ml / 1.4oz	30ml / 1oz

METHOD

Preheat the oven to 175°C (350°F).

In a large bowl, mix the whole wheat flour.

Stir in the grated carrot and finely diced apple.

Add the unsweetened applesauce and beat in the egg. Mix thoroughly, adding water to achieve a muffin batter consistency.

Spoon the batter into a greased muffin tin.

Bake for 20 minutes or until the muffins are golden and firm.

Allow to cool before serving to your dog.

ADVICE

- Choose a sweet variety of apple for natural flavor.

- Ensure the carrots and apples are finely grated or diced for easy digestion.

- These muffins can be stored in the refrigerator for up to 5 days.

SWEET POTATO AND COTTAGE

PREP
20 MIN

COOK
35 MIN

DIFFICULTY
EASY

INGREDIENTS AND QUANTITIES

Ingredients	Puppy (<6 months)	Adult (>6 months-7 years)	Senior (7+ years)
Cooked, mashed sweet potato	100g / 3.5oz	200g / 7oz	150g / 5.3oz
Low-fat cottage cheese	50g / 1.8oz	100g / 3.5oz	75g / 2.6oz
Whole wheat flour	80g / 2.8oz	160g / 5.6oz	120g / 4.2oz
Egg	1 (small)	2 (medium)	1 (small)
Grated carrot	40g / 1.4oz	80g / 2.8oz	60g / 2.1oz
Water	25ml / 0.8oz	50ml / 1.7oz	40ml / 1.4oz

METHOD

Preheat the oven to 180°C (350°F).

In a large bowl, mix the mashed sweet potato and low-fat cottage cheese.

Stir in the whole wheat flour and grated carrot.

Beat the egg and add it to the bowl, then gradually blend in water to achieve a cake-like consistency.

Pour the mixture into a greased cake pan.

Bake for 35 minutes, or until the cake is firm and golden.

Cool before serving to your dog.

ADVICE

- Ensure the sweet potato is cooked until soft and thoroughly mashed.

- Cottage cheese adds protein and calcium but choose a low-fat option to keep it healthier.

- This cake can be refrigerated for up to 4 days.

BEETROOT AND CHICKEN

PREP
20 MIN

COOK
30 MIN

DIFFICULTY
EASY

INGREDIENTS AND QUANTITIES

Ingredients	Puppy (<6 months)	Adult (>6 months-7 years)	Senior (7+ years)
Cooked beetroot, pureed	60g / 2.1oz	120g / 4.2oz	90g / 3.2oz
Ground chicken, cooked	80g / 2.8oz	160g / 5.6oz	120g / 4.2oz
Whole wheat flour	70g / 2.5oz	140g / 4.9oz	105g / 3.7oz
Egg	1 (small)	1 (medium)	1 (small)
Water	20ml / 0.7oz	40ml / 1.4oz	30ml / 1oz

METHOD

Preheat the oven to 180°C (350°F).

In a bowl, mix the pureed beetroot and cooked ground chicken.

Stir in the whole wheat flour.

Beat the egg and add it to the bowl, mixing thoroughly. Gradually add water to achieve a batter consistency.

Spoon the batter into a greased mini cake or muffin tin.

Bake for 30 minutes, or until the cakes are firm and a toothpick inserted comes out clean.

Cool before serving to your dog.

ADVICE

- Make sure the beetroot is cooked and pureed smoothly.

- Use lean ground chicken to keep it healthier.

- These mini cakes can be stored in the refrigerator for up to 5 days.

TURKEY AND PEA POOCH

PREP
15 MIN

COOK
10 MIN

DIFFICULTY
EASY

INGREDIENTS AND QUANTITIES

Ingredients	Puppy (<6 months)	Adult (>6 months-7 years)	Senior (7+ years)
Ground turkey, cooked	50g / 1.8oz	100g / 3.5oz	75g / 2.6oz
Cooked peas	30g / 1oz	60g / 2.1oz	45g / 1.6oz
Whole wheat flour	40g / 1.4oz	80g / 2.8oz	60g / 2.1oz
Egg	1 (small)	1 (medium)	1 (small)
Olive oil	5ml / 0.17oz	10ml / 0.34oz	8ml / 0.27oz
Water	15ml / 0.5oz	30ml / 1oz	25ml / 0.8oz

METHOD

In a bowl, mix the cooked ground turkey and cooked peas.

Stir in the whole wheat flour.

Beat the egg and mix into the turkey and pea mixture. Add water to achieve a pancake batter consistency.

Heat a small amount of olive oil in a frying pan over medium heat.

Pour spoonfuls of the batter into the pan, cooking like pancakes until golden on each side.

Allow to cool before serving to your dog.

ADVICE

- Use lean ground turkey to keep the pancakes healthier.

- Ensure the peas are cooked and mashed for easier digestion.

- Serve these pancakes as a special treat or snack.

BROCCOLI AND BEEF POOCH

PREP
30 MIN

COOK
45 MIN

DIFFICULTY
MODERATE

INGREDIENTS AND QUANTITIES

Ingredients	Puppy (<6 months)	Adult (>6 months-7 years)	Senior (7+ years)
Ground beef, cooked	120g / 4.2oz	240g / 8.5oz	180g / 6.3oz
Chopped broccoli, steamed	50g / 1.8oz	100g / 3.5oz	75g / 2.6oz
Whole wheat flour	100g / 3.5oz	200g / 7oz	150g / 5.3oz
Egg	2 (small)	2 (medium)	2 (small)
Grated carrot	60g / 2.1oz	120g / 4.2oz	90g / 3.2oz
Unsweetened applesauce	40g / 1.4oz	80g / 2.8oz	60g / 2.1oz
Water	35ml / 1.2oz	70ml / 2.4oz	55ml / 1.9oz

METHOD

Preheat the oven to 180°C (350°F).

In a large bowl, mix the cooked ground beef and steamed broccoli.

Add the whole wheat flour, grated carrot, and unsweetened applesauce.

Beat the eggs and blend into the mixture. Gradually add water to achieve a pie-like consistency.

Transfer the mixture into a greased pie or cake pan.

Bake for 45 minutes, or until the pie is golden brown and cooked through.

Cool before serving.

ADVICE

- Choose lean ground beef to keep the pie healthier.

- Ensure the broccoli is cooked and finely chopped.

- This pie can be stored in the refrigerator for up to 4 days.

HARMFUL AND TOXIC INGREDIENTS FOR DOGS

Chocolate: Contains theobromine, which is toxic to dogs.

Caffeine: Even in small quantities it can be dangerous.

Alcohol: Can cause intoxication, coma, and death.

Onions and garlic: Can cause anemia by destroying red blood cells.

Grapes and raisins: Can cause kidney failure.

Artificial sweeteners (such as xylitol): Found in many sweets, chewing gum, and toothpaste, they can cause rapid insulin release and hypoglycemia.

Macadamia nuts: May cause weakness, vomiting, tremors, and hyperthermia.

Bones and Fat: Specially cooked bones can splinter and cause choking or internal injuries, while excessive fats can cause pancreatitis.

Avocado: Contains persin, which can be toxic.

Stone fruits (such as peaches, plums, cherries): Stones can be dangerous, and the fruit itself may contain traces of cyanide.

Milk and dairy products with a high lactose content: Many dogs are lactose intolerant.

Raw eggs: May contain salmonella.

Raw or uncooked meat: May contain harmful bacteria.

Yeasts and doughs: Can expand in the stomach causing pain and potential damage.

Sweets and baked goods: Many contain xylitol or other artificial sweeteners.

Fruit with seeds or stones: As mentioned, some seeds and stones can be toxic.

Very salty foods: Too much salt can lead to health problems.

Spicy foods: Can cause gastrointestinal upset.

Highly fatty foods: Such as bacon and other fatty cuts of meat.

Mushrooms: Some types can be poisonous to dogs.

Foods high in sugar: Can cause obesity and dental problems.

Dried fruit: Some types, such as raisins, are known to be toxic.

Spices and seasonings: Some may be irritating or toxic.

Cook meat well: To eliminate harmful bacteria.

Pay attention to portions: Even healthy foods can be harmful if given in excess.

Consult a veterinarian or pet nutritionist:
Especially if your dog has specific dietary needs or health problems.